PRAISE FOR THIS ROUGH MAGIC

This Rough Magic captures the beauty, complexity, and challenges of life on Portland's Columbia Slough as it winds its way through history and our urban landscape. It is a story of degradation and rejuvenation told by a couple with a keen eye for their furred and feathered co-inhabitants, often relegated to the shadows and margins, but slowly emerging as the slough itself emerges from a century of neglect. Henry and Campbell tell a meditative story that captures the rough magic of this intensively manipulated landscape that still manages to remain wild in the city.

BOB SALLINGER, Urban Conservation Director, Willamette Riverkeeper

While thousands trek in the Gorge and Forest Park, an undiscovered forest and wetland thrives in Portland, hidden behind warehouses and highways. Take a journey with Campbell and Henry into this rough and magical place, where fifteen years ago, the couple decamped to a log cabin among the beavers and egrets. Theirs is a lush tale of learning about, advocating for, and explaining the mysteries of Portland's most hidden natural landscape, the wet and wild Columbia Slough.

LAURA O. FOSTER, author of *Portland Stair Walks*

This reads like a long, warm, engaging letter from home—in this case a home set between the city of Portland and the backwaters of the Columbia River, at the collision point of a hundred years of industrial mayhem and a damaged but resilient natural world. Gracefully written and sharply observed, this book moves beyond suburban naturalism to a place of hope, a vision of where we might start to find our way back to some kind of balance.

KEVIN CANTY, award winning author of *Into the Great Wide Open* and *Nine Below Zero*

This is a lovely and lyrical book—it gets to the heart of how and why we love the wild in our urban spaces. There is awe and wonder and surprise—at the soil and mud and leaves and trees and animals and insects—and also plenty of caution and hurt. It is ambitious and delicious and may well tempt you to seek your own urban wild land home for similar miracles.

SUSAN BARTHEL, Columbia Slough Program Coordinator (ret.), City of Portland

Written with gorgeous prose and filled with personal experiences detailing the good, the bad, and the ugly, *This Rough Magic* gives a true accounting of the issues confronting people and wildlife in an urban watershed. Written by a couple who live beside the Columbia Slough in Portland, OR, the authors detail their journey of discovery, joy and heartbreak honoring the plants and animals, as well as the conflicts and successes in the ongoing quest for balance between the natural and human-centered worlds.

LAURA GUDERYAHN, Ecologist, Portland Parks and Recreation

Poetic, thoughtful and at times even profound, *This Rough Magic* – with illustrations by Amanda Marisa Williams – is a must read for anyone with the slightest interest in Pacific Northwest natural history and good, solid writing.

DAN WEBSTER, Books Editor (ret.), Spokane Spokesman-Review

THIS ROUGH
MAGIC

AT HOME ON THE COLUMBIA SLOUGH

THIS ROUGH
MAGIC

AT HOME ON THE COLUMBIA SLOUGH

Nancy Henry & Bruce Campbell

Illustrated by Amanda Williams

Aristata Press

Library of Congress Control Number: 2023939152

Design & Layout: Anne McClard
Cover Art, Maps and Illustrations: Amanda Marisa Williams
Copy Editing: Sharon AvRutick

ISBN: 979-8-9878524-1-5 (hardcover)
ISBN: 978-1-7362316-9-2 (paperback)
ISBN: 979-8-9878524-0-8 (ebook)

All text, except where noted otherwise, is original to the authors.

Other than the Prologue, this work depicts actual events in the life of the authors as
truthfully as recollection permits and/or can be verified by research. Occasionally,
dialogue consistent with the character or nature of the person speaking has been
supplemented. All persons within are actual individuals; there are no composite
characters. The names of some individuals have been changed to respect their
privacy.

Aristata Press, Portland Oregon
www.aristatapress.com

CONTENTS

For Jeremy Campbell, Willow Crum, and Miranda Acharya. Your love of home, laughter and nature is a constant inspiration.

THE COLUMBIA SLOUGH WATERSHED

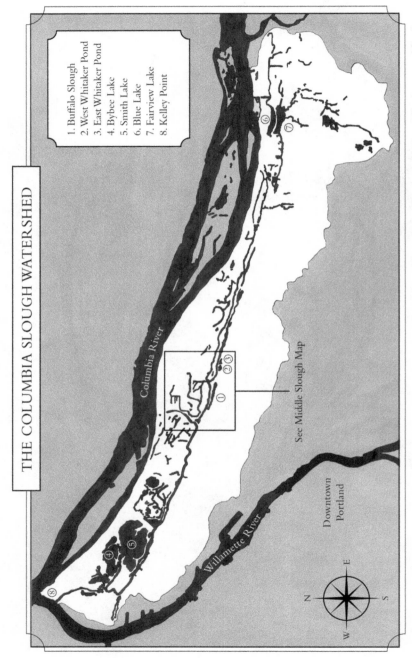

1. Buffalo Slough
2. West Whitaker Pond
3. East Whitaker Pond
4. Bybee Lake
5. Smith Lake
6. Blue Lake
7. Fairview Lake
8. Kelley Point

Columbia River

Willamette River

Downtown
Portland

See Middle Slough Map

N
E
W
S

Adapted from: City of Portland, Bureau of Environmental Services

THE MIDDLE SLOUGH

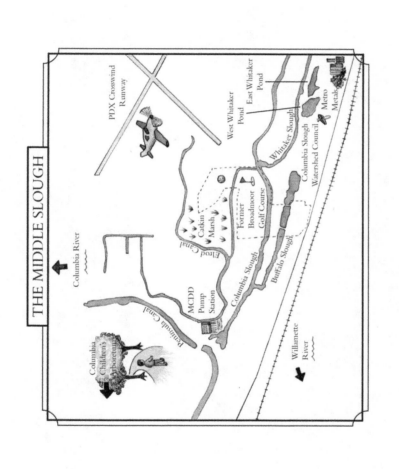

Columbia River

PDX Crosswind Runway

West Whitaker Pond

East Whitaker Pond

Whitaker Slough

Metro
Metak...

Columbia Slough
Watershed Council

Catkin Marsh

Former Broadmoor Golf Course

Elrod Canal

Columbia Slough

Buffalo Slough

MCDD Pump Station

Peninsula Canal

Columbia Children's Arboretum

Willamette River

PROLOGUE · COLUMBIA RIVER FLOODPLAIN

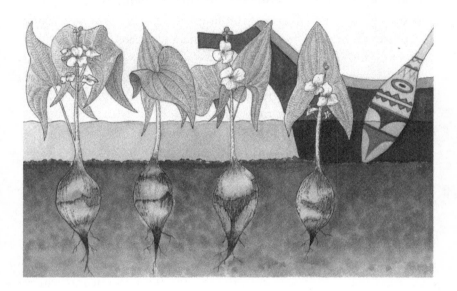

SEPTEMBER 1820

The Chinookan woman slipped from her small cedar canoe into the pond, holding the side for balance until her feet touched silt. Cold water lapped her thighs and sent a shiver into her belly. A sign of first frost and longer nights to come. She glanced at the three cottonwoods on the marshy south shore to confirm her location. Earlier in the summer, she had sheared from the surface a clutch of wapato leaves for stew greens. Now she's returned for the plant's rich, nutritious tubers, under thick stalks anchored in the muck. In the coming years, white settlers would name these bulbs "duck potatoes."

The woman had a method for rooting out wapato tubers from water that ran high. Her thin arms couldn't manage heavy digging sticks in deeper water. The sticks also churned up too much mud. Instead, she used her agile big toes to kick roots from the muck, while she pulled the stalks with one hand and held onto the dugout with the other. Foot cramps slowed her at first, but soon her toes limbered. Feeling the satisfying crunch of roots giving way, she smiled as several tubers popped to the surface, dense balls of goodness for her fire. She grabbed the limp stalks, shook off the water and threw the muddy roots into the horsetail basket at the bottom of the dugout.

This wapato patch was thick, so the sun had swung to the west by the time she filled her basket. Climbing back into the boat, she wiped her forehead and massaged her feet, driving her fingers between her toes.

As the cold season approached, the woman and her village were ready. Wapato in the ponds and marshlands was plentiful, unlike last season when the muskrat mamas whelped many babies. The rodents had gobbled up the plant's snowy flowers and tender leaves before diving down for the roots. This year, her coyote friends had helped curb the muskrats. Tonight, she would roast some of today's harvest over an open fire. The rest she would dry on a reed mat and pound into dense, rich flour to pat into cakes with deer fat or mix with dried huckleberries and acorns.

This season, the big river nearby had also provided hundreds of fat spring salmon which were already racked and dried for winter, along with dozens of giant sturgeons pulled from these ponds. When the frost arrived, the families would move into their winter lodges on the southern ridge upland from the big river. The woman looked forward to the cold season when many families shared a long cedar plank house, their sleeping mats clustered along opposite sides. She relished the slower pace and social time gathering with other women around a central hearth.

The woman would easily find her mate in the next season and go on to birth three healthy children in five years. But before her oldest could claim his animal spirit, disaster wiped out their village and pushed the only adult survivors to make the long walk east to a village in the high desert. No famine decimated her clan of river dwellers in this resource-rich place, where winters were mild, and fish, clams, game, roots, and berries were plentiful. Nor did a war erupt between the Chinookan tribes that dotted both shores of the Wimal or "Big Water." Instead, in 1830, a "cold sick" swept through Neerchokikoo, the woman's village, taking away more than 90 percent of its people. Anglo historians attribute this mass die-off of Columbia River Native peoples to smallpox, influenza, or perhaps even "virgin soil" malaria, so named because indigenous peoples had no previous contact with the disease. They were defenseless against these maladies.

INTRODUCTION • THE ADVENTURE BEGINS

" Slough: pronounced *sloo*. A wetland, swamp, or slow-moving body of water, often seasonal or a side channel of a river. Also: a mental state of sadness and hopelessness—or moral degradation.

" Slough: pronounced *sluff*. A mass or layer of dead tissue separated from the surrounding tissue, or anything that is shed or cast off.

FRANTIC CRIES outside our house woke us one recent dawn: a series of loud barks followed by a short howl. It was a coyote, screeching in terrible pain. Perhaps caught in a trap?

Running out to investigate, we looked east into the dim light. The coyote was fifty yards off, pacing back and forth over a freshly bulldozed mound of dirt. We'd seen this one before. She was the mother of four pups. In the evenings, the pups played close by, leaping atop a large, galvanized drainage pipe, and sliding off into a tangle of dandelions, thistles, and goldenrod. Occasionally other adult coyotes gathered to observe the frolics. Family day at a canine amusement park.

Now we watched as the mother paced and howled frantically. No pups anywhere. Were they lost? Were they dead? A few gun-owning neighbors who let their cats out sometimes took shots at coyotes.

Living on the Columbia Slough, we often hear coyotes. Especially at night. Howls, barks, yelps, and yips echo from afar—or from right outside our bedroom window. We can't always decode the racket. Maybe it's *Let's hang out and howl at the moon.* Or *I just snagged a muskrat—wanna join me for dinner?*

What we heard now was an unmistakable cry of anguish, a universal expression of grief recognizable to any species within earshot. *My heart is broken!*

After several minutes, she fell silent and trotted off, disappearing into the high grass. For a few days afterward, we kept an eye out for her and the pups. No coyotes appeared to jump the drainage pipe, though one evening the crows showed up in force to hector a brush rabbit, darting down to peck its head and drive it in all directions.

The Columbia Slough supports abundant wildlife. Surrounded by industry, slough critters endure the flash and thunder of human activity, clinging to a frail lifeline of streams, channels, and brushy cover. Animals shelter in the sparse forests adjoining the nearby airport, make their homes in shrinking wetlands and stagnant waterways. They tuck themselves into concrete culverts, snoop around warehouses, and pop up in residential neighborhoods.

Slough wildlife walk a crooked trail between conflict and coexistence with humans.

And it is always present. A quick look out our window confirms this. Cormorants perch on shoreline snags and air out their wings. Kestrels hover over grassy swales. Downy woodpeckers flit around the suet feeder. Silver-spotted tiger moths flutter, swallows swoop, mourning doves coo, and dragonflies dart about like Sopwith Camels. The show never stops.

As we approach two decades living beside the slough, the wildlife has never ceased to surprise us. Sometimes the surprises are heartbreaking. Speeding traffic near our house kills many animals. Raccoons, rabbits, and birds are common casualties. Also, northern flickers, a flagship woodpecker in the Pacific Northwest. Once a fawn curled in the median, hit trying to cross the road along the Elrod Canal. Another time, a large red-tailed hawk, whose wings spanned a full meter and fluffed in the breeze above its carcass for days. One day on a bike ride, we discovered a dead stoat lying perfectly preserved on the roadside, its soft butterscotch belly facing skyward.

Despite the frequent road kills, slough animals don't squash easily. They evade eviction notices from a host of human landlords. Just in time, they flee from advancing bulldozers and steam shovels to return at nightfall and reclaim their homes.

The persistence of wildlife under great pressure in this area is part of the reason we wrote this book. We wanted to learn how the slough's overtaxed ecosystem hosts so many animals, plants, and people.

At times the slough was a conundrum. A bewildering, improbable menagerie of mammals, reptiles, amphibians, insects, and birds. Where do all these critters sleep? What do they eat? How do they protect their young? In Shakespeare's *The Tempest*, Prospero used "rough magic" to bend the fractious spirits of nature to his will. His touch, transforming the mundane into the miraculous, is clearly reflected in and around the human-manipulated waters of the Columbia Slough.

Researching the slough, it's easy to get lost in the weeds.

Rescue came in the advice of Miss Frizzle (the teacher in *The Magic School Bus*): "Take chances! Make mistakes! Get messy!" she tells her students. "If you keep asking questions, you'll keep getting answers."

So, we've gotten messy. Mixing it up with the mud and mosquitoes is one way we've gotten to know the slough. No reference book could replace the intimacy we've gained from years of on-the-ground and in-the-water observations. We've used our home base to full advantage. Watching. Listening. Smelling. Tasting. Scratching. Staying silent. Waiting . . . until a doorstep discovery transfixes us with an aha moment—or befuddles us with more questions.

Our DIY outdoor school has been slow work over slow water, which took some getting used to, but eventually our metabolic rates synched with the slough's drowsy flow. We were blessed as well with unexpected gifts of "spooky action at a distance," a phrase Albert Einstein coined to explain how subatomic particles —even when light-years apart—could link up and exchange information instantaneously. Einstein called this mind-bender quantum entanglement. Communication without a wasted nanosecond.

Maybe quantum entanglement explained our empathy for the plight of the mother coyote. Traveling at the hyper-speed of raw emotion, her full-throated grief bridged the gulf between our species. In that moment, our world became entangled with hers.

* * *

WRITING THIS BOOK TOGETHER, we wanted to make room for both our voices. And it was clear early on that at times the ways we saw, felt, or interpreted our environment clashed. So we settled on alternating authorship of chapters, each with a first-person approach. Nancy (who's rarely seen a body of water she didn't want to swim) highlighted hearth and home, and dove into slough history, water, neighborhood, and sediment issues. Bruce, a lifelong gardener and hiker, explored the plants, animals, habitats, and surrounding mini-verse of ecological eccentricities.

Over many breakfast discussions, we worked to balance our perspectives and resolve differences in memories, doing our best to report events accurately. Our hope is that this collaboration reflects the awe that two very different people share for this unique and fragile locale we've embraced.

1 BESOTTED BY WATER (2008)

> **All water has a perfect memory and is forever trying to get back to where it was.**

TONI MORRISON, 1986 SPEECH

. . .

"Forget about flood insurance," said Mark, shaking his head. "Even if you could get it. Not worth the cost."

Mark is our realtor and friend, a no-nonsense erstwhile Alaskan fisherman. He stood between Bruce and me, the three of us gazing at the slough, a wide band of wind-rippled water about sixty feet away.

Mark pointed toward the Columbia River, hands shading his eyes like a pioneer explorer. "There's the Marine Drive levee a couple of miles north and a pump system along the slough. You shouldn't have to worry about floods...I think."

Mark's tone did not exactly reassure. I'd grown up on coastal waterways in the South. More than once, I'd hoisted furniture off carpets soaked in hurricane-driven river water. When I was a kid, flood insurance was not part of my lexicon. Now prospective-homeowner-with-future-mortgage-me felt a sharp stab of doubt that we could keep our noses above water here.

"So what are you saying?" I asked. "We're safe from floods, right?" But Mark had walked on.

Mark was our agent and the seller's agent, too. The property had been listed for well over a year. These two red flags were in the back of my mind as we walked the property on a bright midsummer day. I did my best to ignore them.

Bruce wanted to assess the sunlight exposure for a permaculture garden he imagined. He planned to make use of all dynamic inputs—water, soil, sunshine, plants, animals, insects—to garden sustainably, using a method he'd developed as an environmental educator at an alternative high school. Over two decades, Bruce had led students in habitat restoration projects in the Columbia Gorge and throughout the Pacific Northwest. In 2002, they'd studied the environmental history of the Columbia River, a three-week field experience that took thirty-six students and four educators (including me), on a two-thousand-mile road trip from Astoria to the Canadian border.

Permaculture practices promised more productivity from less-than-ideal plots, like the half acre we were walking with Mark. I hoped this fact would sway Bruce toward the property.

Bruce pointed to the northeast corner near the slough. "That's our sunniest spot. It'll get five hours, maybe a little more. Just barely enough for tomatoes." He didn't look thrilled.

And I was surprised. How could the north side be the sunniest?

He indicated the cluster of tall cedars above the south yard, which would block light in the afternoon. Critical hours for sun-loving vegetables.

"At least it's a one-story house," he said, answering my unasked question. "Sun's above the roof in the summer."

I glanced at Bruce's face, half-shrouded under a ball cap, primed for any sign he saw and felt what I did. I'd already fallen in love with this log house nestled among cottonwoods at the end of a dirt road hugging the slough's southern edge. Dodging potholes down to a home perched above a wide ribbon of water took me back to a childhood living beside rivers and lakes.

In the living room, I'd plopped down on the homeowners' floral couch and looked out the picture window. Ducks and geese circled over the water. I knew little about the slough beyond how to spell and pronounce the word. But the comforting sight of water evoked sultry summers spent swimming, gigging frogs, and catching crawdads.

The next day we made an offer.

* * *

Twelve years later, I stand on our dock over the Buffalo Slough, looking toward the "Big Water" Columbia River. It's summer 2020 and air traffic is light. At the airport's southern perimeter a mile away, rows of Alaska Airlines jets line out wing to wing, grounded by COVID. Two miles north, the river curls around Broughton Beach. We now grow vegetables where two hundred years ago, Chinookan peoples, like the woman that I imagined, dug wapato from the ponds that dotted this floodplain. She would have lived in one of dozens of villages perched on the fertile lands bracketed by the Willamette River to the west, the Sandy River to the east, and the Columbia River to the north. These villages shared a common Chinookan language but were given many names by the white people who arrived in force on the heels of Lewis and Clark.

Wappato, Multnomah, Kathlamet, Clackamas, Chinook, Tualatin, Kalapuya, and Molalla were a few of these Anglicized names. The record bears scant evidence that Native Americans in this area used any of them.

The Buffalo Slough, where Bruce and I make our home, is a southern side channel of the nineteen-mile-long Columbia Slough. Our half-acre property spans the midpoint of this snaking waterway. Just over nine miles to our east, the slough begins at Fairview Lake. It ends 9.8 miles west of us, spilling out at Kelley Point, where the Willamette and Columbia Rivers merge.

Decades ago, when I taught irregular English pronunciations, I would often ask seventh graders, "How many words can you think of in which the letters 'ough' have a different sound?" In no time, they'd call out "rough," "though," "through," "bough," and "bought." But never "slough."

Not so common, these words slough *(sloo)* and slough *(sluff)*. They are heteronyms—words that are spelled the same but hold different meanings. Unlike homophones, heteronyms are also pronounced differently. Ironic that the *sluff* version of "slough" also fits the slough waterways. For most of its history, the Columbia Slough was treated as something dead, "to be shed or cast off"—a sluggish flush toilet for a growing city.

The Columbia Slough teems with life. It's also degraded and polluted. From our deck, we've watched river otters train their pups to crack mussels and chomp crayfish, rolling comically onto their backs to chew their catch. We've logged dozens of bird species on and around the water, including many generations of great blue herons who squawk their claim to the Buffalo's north shore. We call them all "Gus."

On the slope above Gus's perch, a succession of trees, mostly cottonwoods, have died and decayed prematurely, snags crashing down one after the other into the water. Older residents told us a dairy farmer buried spent fuel cans on that slope in the 1950s to extend his domain further over the water. On that same spot we'd watched a landscaping contractor saturate blackberry bushes with herbicide.

A motley collection of human occupants and stakeholders are

connected to the Columbia Slough. At times their interests clash, and public meetings erupt in loud, polarized shouting matches. In our area of the middle slough alone, the Portland International Airport, the fifty-four–bed Columbia River Correctional Institution, the Oregon Food Bank, the Oregon Department of Environmental Quality (DEQ), Dignity Village (a tiny home encampment for Portland's unhoused population), the Columbia Slough Watershed Council, three golf courses, dozens of small and large businesses, and a few hundred renters and homeowners claim space. Dozens of vehicle and tent dwellers crowd the roadsides. Most all would agree that a cleaned-up, vibrant slough is a worthy goal. But full recovery of this complex watershed remains a long-term, expensive endeavor. And in the official jargon, always "subject to change." I may dream of clear, fast water, but the slough dream itself is a slow one. It's a dream achieved in increments, section by section, slope by slope, year by year.

2 IN SEARCH OF HOOTERVILLE

City people make most of the fuss about the charms of country life.

MASON COOLEY, *CITY APHORISMS*

. . .

WE MOVED next to the Columbia Slough in the fall of 2008. The long and winding path to our new zip code in Portland's Sunderland neighborhood consumed two years of look-sees, but now we owned a mid-twentieth-century log house. It wasn't exactly our dream house, but Nancy was sold on it.

"I want to be carried feet first out of here," she announced.

Gardening had always been close to my heart, so I sized up our surroundings more critically, seeing little potential for amber waves of grain or corn as high as an elephant's eye. We were next to the Broadmoor Golf Course. To ensure green, weed-free fairways, the groundskeepers depended heavily upon chemicals. Pollution from garages, factories, and big trucks added more woes to the neighborhood. Commerce dominated the Sunderland, clustering around the slough like animals at an African waterhole.

Putting down stakes in the industrial heart of the city wasn't our first choice. We'd originally sought a country house with a short commute to Portland. We fantasized a preserved-in-amber kind of life, a Hooterville replete with general store next to a post office. Nothing too precious. Just a few good green acres to plant carrots and kale, pak choi and spinach.

Though the Sunderland had a wild vibe to it, it was no happy romping ground for the likes of Lassie or Old Yeller. Too much industrial traffic. Too many cyclone fences. Still, the neighborhood's shopworn appearance didn't put us off. We saw the rough makings of a home here. When a friend damned our new location with faint praise, I had no ready elevator speech to pitch its benefits. At the time, I wasn't convinced there was much to brag about.

"Things here look a little . . . scruffy," was his weak attempt at tact. "I heard the Columbia Slough is full of frogs with two heads."

Har-har. Two-headed frogs. An old joke. Still many Portlanders considered the slough a repository of historical horrors, a habitat better suited for Jenny Greenteeth, an English water-demon with wild hair, green skin, and ghastly fangs. According to legend, Jenny dragged children into the neighborhood swamp and drowned them.

The slough harbored no water demons. Its demons were born of industry. Heavy metals and forever chemicals. Trapped in the muck, they lodged in the soft tissues of birds, fish, and humans. But even though it was no place for a summer dip, the slough softened the hard edges of the Sunderland. Cocktail hours also helped.

In the evenings, Nancy and I poured strong drinks and sat outside, catching whiffs of mud and rotting algae. Animal life surrounded us. The setting sun brought to life a concert of crickets and bullfrogs. A beaver slapped his tail on the water. Two raccoons hissed and growled in the willows, working out territorial disputes. A blue heron sounded from the yellow-flag irises on the north side. K-A-A-A-RK!

Soon we realized we'd lucked into in a vest-pocket Valhalla with its own private zoo—or backyard wildlife refuge. The slough seemed to muster some sleight-of-hand sorcery to call forth the spirits of nature. Evening breezes riffled the indolent waters; overhanging branches swayed and creaked. The sun varnished the treetops, giving a sufurous glow to the cottonwoods and conifers.

In the morning hours, the boisterous wildlife sounded like a neighborhood garage band, at times drowning out the Sunderland's heavy-metal philharmonic of planes, cars, trucks, and trains. On blustery days, trees bent in the westerly breeze, broadcasting a hit parade of birdsong. Robins, red-winged blackbirds, yellow-rumped warblers, flickers, black-capped chickadees. The crows and blue jays joined in with their corvid karaoke, their squawks and screeches silencing the songbirds.

Even with winter approaching, plenty of wildlife headed our way. The slough remained a hotspot of animal activity. All that was missing was the *Song of the South* soundtrack with Uncle Remus belting out "Zip-a-dee-doo-dah/zip-a-dee-ay/My, oh my, what a wonderful day."

One afternoon I phoned Nancy at her office in an educational consulting firm. As expected, her tone was curt. She was always busy. Personal phone calls were only for emergencies. But I needed to announce that a river otter was dozing on our dock. "That lazy layabout is warming his belly in the sun," I said. "I had no idea otters lived on the slough. I thought the water wasn't clean enough."

The wildlife bedazzled our daughter's boyfriend. With binoculars, he tracked a raptor hunting the slough. The shrill whistles of the red-tailed hawk sounded from the treetops. A short first note—then a long second note. One day, he watched our local great blue heron, Gus, drive off a snowy egret. Nearby, a belted kingfisher dove repeatedly from a snag to snatch up minnows and aquatic insects, its loud chitter belying its tininess. Even the less spectacular stuff got his attention. Shaking his head as he watched a clutch of voles dart out from the bushes to devour sunflower seeds beneath the bird feeder, he told our daughter she was lucky to live in Disney World.

Miranda laughed. "That's not Minnie Mouse and her friends. Real animals aren't cartoon characters."

The slough wasn't quite the *Wild Kingdom*, yet it held more wildness than most nature parks we'd visited. Unfortunately, real animals cause real damage. They dug beneath the foundation of our home, gnawed on the log siding, and set up shop inside the chimney. Moles, mice, carpenter ants, beetles, squirrels, starlings. Fungus and mold infested the crawl space and uncaulked crevices. Mother Nature took big bites out of our dwelling. We lived in a biodegradable house. Our ringside seat to the slough's five-star nature show came with a steep admission price.

Nancy and I reflected often on how we'd relocated to an alternate universe only a few miles from our former home. For nineteen years we'd owned a six-bedroom bungalow in Northeast Portland. A child's ball toss from a mortuary and a Kentucky Fried Chicken, the drafty old home admitted the sooty stink from crematorium smokestacks along with the smell of drumsticks frying in hot oil. Source material for predictable crispy critter jokes.

After selling that house, we rented for two years. Looking for the ideal property within our budget was soul sucking. Promising acreage usually included a vermin-infested house with a gone-to-brambles barn. We couldn't afford to shell out a half million for property, then another half million to build or remodel a small home. Nothing affordable we looked at had what Scottish poet James Thomson called "the whistling music of the lagging plough."

Out-of-staters with deep pockets wanted what we wanted: Land. Lots of it. We couldn't compete financially with this madding crowd, so we opted for the Rust Belt rustic of Portland's Sunderland neighborhood, four miles and across the tracks from downtown.

We were only dimly aware that the slough hadn't existed until the early twentieth century. Engineered for commercial activity, it was a channel carved from the heart of the Columbia River floodplain. Our little log house was perched on filled-in wetlands. On stolen Indian land. Like us, the slough was new to the neighborhood, but it had senior status. It had survived the Industrial Age's school of hard knocks, a time when Euro-Americans cut down the old growth forests to build the foundation for a boom-and-bust cash economy. Back in that day, no kayakers photographed bushtits perched on a willow branch. The slough was a malodorous swamp, a place for decent folks to avoid. Farms, dairies, factories, and slaughterhouses populated the floodplain. Cows, pigs, goats, and sheep proliferated. Tugboats, barges, and garbage clogged the slough. It was an open sewer brimming with toxic chemicals, a place of ecological misery. Along with all the filth, prosperity gushed from the open spigot of frontier capitalism, enabling Portland to become the city it is today.

Throughout it all, the slough survived. It still had a detectable heartbeat, though it bore visible and invisible scars. The invisible ones were what worried us the most. The poisons of the past were locked into land and water, into the bodies of living creatures. PCBs damaged livers. Chlordane caused seizures. Mercury hallucinations and death. Etc., etc., etc. In search of Hooterville, had we landed in Polluterville? A list of the slough's toxins could fill an old-time phone book.

Over the last several decades, many advocates have stepped up to help, including public-spirited individuals and neighborhood groups, government agencies, businesses, and nonprofit organizations. The Columbia Slough Watershed Council—and its many passionate community partners—now protects the floodplain from "pollution, rampant development, and loss of open space." They have all worked hard to repair the damage, accomplishing great feats. Many garbage dumps were removed. Raw sewage no longer befouls the water. Birds and mammals thrive in reconstituted wetlands. Federal and state laws restrict industrial incursions.

And yet, the real world still prevails, putting public lands at risk. At night, we catch the chemical stench from smokestacks and the burned rubber smell of street racers. The deadly seesaw contest between human nature and Mother Nature often throws the ecosystems of the slough out of balance. A short walk along desolate sections of the slough confirms this fact. Your eyes, ears, and nose don't ever lie. In the seventeenth century, John Milton claimed that humans "live like Nature's bastards, not her sons." Too many of us still do.

The slough has survived over a century of egregious abuses. Its health has improved, but not enough. In his book *When Veins Ignite: Either Integration or Degradation,* neuroscientist Abhijit Naskar says: "If we don't have a place for nature in our heart, how can we expect nature to have a place for us?"

Staying close to the city, Nancy and I grudgingly admitted, made more ecological sense than living in the countryside. Less driving. More public transportation. Better bicycle lanes and access to services. For us, it became a false either/or binary. City life was no ecotopia— rats, cockroaches, pigeons, and squirrels who didn't know their place. But the environmental excesses of living in the sticks often gut the natural world and accelerate climate change. When our killer ape ancestors fled East Africa approximately sixty thousand years ago, their carbon footprint was very small. Now ours is Godzilla-sized—wherever or however we live.

Our decision to stay in the city was based on other considera-tions as well. For us, the great outdoors was still a necessity, but tourism had converted much of rural America into a travesty of idle curiosities, its repurposed spaces too often packed tight with tchotchke shops, dude ranches, roadside animal zoos, and gilded getaways for the wealthy. We didn't blame the people who had lived there for generations. They were the victims of Wall Street high rollers who stripped the land of resources, outsourced their jobs and then forgot about them. The global economy had hollowed out Hooterville, leaving behind too many shuttered storefronts, clear-cut forests, and angry young men with bad haircuts and drug addictions.

Unexpectedly, something else helped squash our desire to escape the city: Advertising. Madison Avenue has wrested control of how we relate to Mother Nature. More than ever, corporate commercials manipulate public attitudes about country life, fostering dangerous fantasies of abundance, privilege, and over-consumption. According to the manufacturers of misinformation, we can't enjoy the splendors of the great outdoors unless we buy expensive merchandise, consume the right prescription drugs, and rip-up endangered habitats with our offroad vehicles. This sort of advertising puts a happy face on ecocide. A happy face that acts like a mutating virus, infecting us with complacency and weak-ening our defenses against the commodification of the natural world. Despite our determination to resist this virus, we had doubts whether we could maintain full immunity to it. People were always trying to escape something. Wars. Plagues. Family. Friends. Taxes. Bill collectors. We recalled what the movie character Buckaroo Banzai said: "No matter where you go, there you are."

I've yet to see a glitzy commercial that encourages people to live large on a place like the Columbia Slough. Too bad, because living here offers enough entertainment (and spiritual solace) to take the sting out of modern life. Just take a look around and you'll see little brown myotis bats performing acrobatic arabesques while gobbling up clouds of black gnats. At sunset, goldfinches dabble their butts in birdbaths, keeping an eye out for the neighbor's cat. Swallowtail butterflies mob the milkweed while eluding a red-breasted robin. The energetic congress of wildlife commands water, land, and sky. Honking and quacking. Chittering and buzzing. Croaking, snorting, and howling. Living and dying. It's all free. No need to make a big buy, pop pills, or swill beer for a Rocky Mountain high.

Nancy was right that we'd found our forever home. From the moment we moved in, we wanted to protect it and the good things we discovered about the slough. Searching for nature in the coun-try, we found it curled up into the concrete cracks of the Sunder-land neighborhood. Getting a spider bite or hornet sting didn't require a drive to a wilderness sanctuary. Neither did seeing ospreys and red-breasted nuthatches or watching a pack of coyotes trot across a meadow.

Adjusting to life here was a process, but we benefited from the sadder but wiser wisdom of hindsight, taking to heart Wendell Berry's words, "You can best serve civilization by being against what usually passes for it."

For us, it's about reverence of place. Creating artificial barriers between civilization and the wildness of the world isn't natural. Every neighborhood—especially urban ones—should be rewilded. Why not integrate the natural world into every aspect of our lives? Why burn gasoline or kilowatts to drive hundreds of miles to visit national parks, eat bad food at concession restaurants, purchase trinkets, and gawk at remnant buffalo herds and surviving wolves or grizzly bears?

Nancy and I found our own special kind of country living smack dab in the industrial heart of the city. Trying to grow our garden, we work the soil and support the natural world any way we can. It's not nearly enough to save the planet, yet the curative powers of nature bring us into closer communion with everything that crawls, flies, skitters, and swims. Animals are all around us, and from where we sit, they seem more than ready to reoccupy the commons.

3 A BRIEF HISTORY OF THE SLOUGH

> **The only thing that stops God from sending another flood is that the first one was useless.**

NICOLAS CHAMFORT, "MAXIMES ET PENSEES"

. . .

BEFORE THE TWENTIETH CENTURY, the Columbia River often flooded its banks. Floodwaters spread through grassy bottomlands, at times reaching far enough to lap the base of a hill two miles south. Columbia Boulevard, the main artery of Portland's industrial corridor, now tops this rise, amid the constant din of truck traffic. Devastating to humans, these floods nonetheless recharged aquifers and enriched the floodplain with a cornucopia of nutrients.

Before the dams—before the draining, dredging, filling, and re-engineering of the Columbia River floodplain—spring freshets cut new channels through the wetlands each year, depositing thick layers of silt. This fertile soil nourished generations of Chinookan peoples who fished from small boats and gathered wapato, water plantain, and other plants from seasonal ponds and lakes.

Today's Columbia Slough bears little resemblance to the historic floodplain. Early in the twentieth century, Portland burgeoned into a small city, seeking to shed its seedy "Stumptown" image. As urban development expanded east of the Willamette River, farmers, ranchers, and industry moved north onto unclaimed wetlands in the Columbia watershed. Easy access to the river and side streams soon attracted slaughterhouses, stockyards, dairies, and lumber mills.

But the river continued to seasonally flood the lowlands, throwing a wrench into land use expansion. In 1917, area landowners united to conquer the floodplain. Dividing the area into three contiguous districts, they drained and filled the wetlands and side channels. They built dikes and levees to hold the river back from their farms, orchards, and stockyards. They deepened one main east–west channel into a nineteen-mile navigable stream, clearing the way for tugboats to move logs westward from tree-felling sites in East County to the mills on the lower slough. Today's main slough channel is that dredged and engineered waterway. It's the tamed child of commerce and transportation.

New meatpacking plants siphoned slough water to clean their cuts of cattle and sheep before packaging. Eventually, these plants were discharging as much as 150,000 pounds of blood, guts, and animal parts into the slough each day. Though disgusting to picture, animal wastes were the least of the slough's accumulating troubles. Bones, blood, and skin, after all, are organic and eventually decompose.

Much of the sewage from the city of Portland also flowed straight into the slough, via brick and concrete pipes laid for that purpose. Eventually this sludge discharged into the Willamette River. By the mid-1930s the Willamette was so oxygen deprived that salmon fingerlings died minutes after immersion. River swimming was banned. In November 1938, four thousand schoolchildren rallied at City Hall to protest Willamette River pollution and demand change.

In those years, the slough's appalling conditions attracted little outrage. It was normal then for sewage "treatment" to consist simply of conveying raw wastes to natural bodies of water to be diluted and dissipated. But with most of its feeder streams and side channels drained and filled-in, the steady onslaught of sewage clogged the slough. The rich fish, bird, and plant habitats in the Columbia floodplain that had supported millennia of Native Americans were fast disappearing.

In 1920 city leaders tried to speed up the slough's flow to flush accumulated sewage more efficiently out to the Willamette River. They dredged the mile-long Peninsula Canal from the Columbia River south, T-boning into the main slough at its midpoint near Elrod Road. But silt repeatedly plugged the canal, and the city re-dredged it multiple times. Then 1948's Vanport Flood choked off the canal completely, and the city washed its hands of the effort (pun intended). Today, the legacy of that failure, the Peninsula Canal is a placid landlocked backwater with homes and pastures of sheep and goats on the west slope and a men's prison, golf course, and tiny-house village on the east.

Through the first half of the twentieth century, the slough remained a cesspool. More lumber mills and wood product manufacturers moved in, followed by truck freight and transportation companies. For the next half century, the St. Johns Landfill smothered the lower slough wetlands in mountainous loads of Portland's postwar trash.

The new Portland International Airport (PDX) was

constructed in 1941 along the middle slough. It replaced Swan Island Municipal Airport, its runways too short to handle larger jet traffic. Where wapato patches once grew and giant sturgeons swam, asphalt spread over tons of fill dirt to support heavy aircraft. PDX eventually claimed three thousand acres of Columbia River floodplain.

On Memorial Day in 1948 a railroad embankment used as a dike gave way, weakened from weeks of high water in the Columbia River. A torrent rushed into the lower slough, destroying Vanport's public housing project, an intentional community created for wartime shipbuilding. The flood left over eighteen thousand people homeless. Black-and-white photos of our own street show several homes flooded to the roofline. Floodwaters ripped away wooden framing from our home, still under construction at the time, sending wood floating off into the swollen Buffalo Slough.

By midcentury the slough was so polluted that lumber mill workers balked at handling logs slimed with meatpacking, hog farming, and other wastes. Finally, in the 1950s, city leaders built the Columbia Boulevard Wastewater Treatment Plant, which was fed by a maze of collection pipes and pump stations. For the first time in Portland, raw sewage was treated before discharge into the Columbia River. The practice of household sewage flowing directly into rivers was finally ending.

For another forty years, though, the slough remained a dumping ground for agriculture and industry. Well into the 1990s, more than two hundred industries emptied their wastes into slough waterways. Pesticides from golf courses and farms that lined the upper and middle sloughs joined heavy metals and other poisons from the lower slough's industries, and all drained into the waterways. Slough banks were fouled with toxic slime.

John Bonebrake lived near the slough for eighty years. Born in 1910, he recalled the waters of his childhood in an interview with environmental historian Ellen Stroud, for her 1999 article: "Troubled Waters in Ecotopia: Environmental Racism in Portland, Oregon."

"I remember it in my mind as a nice, little wavy slough," Bonebrake told Stroud. He described cottonwood trees lining the water-way, and a dozen or so smaller sloughs and marshes connecting to the Columbia River. He recalled hunting owls, finding arrowheads, and fishing and swimming a short walk from his childhood home.

Now Bonebrake said, "It's nothing but a stagnant, stale, smelly stream."

Today, most Portlanders who live near the slough are middle and lower income. Many are immigrants and people of color. After the Vanport Flood, African Americans and other displaced shipyard workers were settled into nearby neighborhoods, redlined from relocating farther into the city. Today, tent dwellers and newcomers sometimes fish the slough to supplement their diets, despite posted signs near fishing spots: "Warning: The Columbia Slough Is Polluted." The signs are printed in twelve languages. Colorful illustrations drive the message home: DON'T swim in the water, DON'T drink the water, and DON'T eat the fish.

Much has improved on the slough since Stroud published her essay, yet the long shadow of our ancestors' industry lingers still.

4 WHO SPEAKS FOR THE SLOUGH?

" If I were a tree, I would have no reason to love a human.

MAGGIE STIEFVATER, *THE RAVEN BOYS*

. . .

EATING LUNCH, I decide to take a look at a 2019 Portland's Bureau of Environmental Services (BES) report card on the health of the Columbia Slough. Nancy had read it already and put it in front of me. The report card isn't good. You'd want to hide it from your parents. *Habitat: D-. Fish & Wildlife: F.* The slough has low oxygen levels—and sedimentary deposits of toxins. Were things really that awful?

I look northeast out an open window. The slough is a little low, exposing a large expanse of mud, but things look okay. Lots of ducks and cormorants. I can hear a kingfisher chittering along the shoreline, the trill of a red-winged blackbird in a cottonwood. A few days earlier, I saw a raptor winging across the slough, a snake writhing in its talons. If any of these birds had read the BES report card, they weren't overly concerned.

I have no argument with the environmental scientists who compiled the hard facts about the state of the slough. They did their homework, conducted tests, and came up with the damning data. But if this wildlife habitat is degraded to an alarming degree, why don't river otters, crayfish, and caddisflies just give up the ghost?

To stretch my legs after a morning at the computer, I decide to investigate the invisible. I can't see toxins or low oxygen levels, but I can observe plants and animals. What grows here? What parts of the habitat still have a heartbeat? The Catkin Marsh, which flanks the northwest side of the golf course, seems a good place to find answers.

It's a slow day on the Broadmoor. Not many golfers about. I walk about a mile, crossing greens and fairways. Douglas firs, ponderosas, and giant sequoias cast deep shade on the short-cropped grass, but in other places, the locusts and birches admit enough sunlight to give the golf course a pastoral shimmer.

Near the main slough shore, I come across a pile of freshwater mussel shells. For a tasty snack, a raccoon probably dug these macroinvertebrates from their burrows in the mud. The shells look like floaters *(Anodonta spp.)*. Freshwater mussels play a gigantic role in maintaining water quality by filtering out impurities. Their shells provide a slow-release source of calcium, phosphorous, and nitrogen. In the Pacific Northwest—and elsewhere—freshwater mussel populations are dwindling rapidly. Blame it on the usual culprits. Industrial development, recreational activities, and people building houses too close to water.

According to the BES report card, the slough is also suffering a steep decline of macroinvertebrate bottom-dwelling insects. All aquatic macroinvertebrates weave themselves into the food web. Lose them and everything unravels.

Myriad macroinvertebrates inhabit the slough. While I go about my business, they go about theirs. Dragonflies, freshwater mussels, and crayfish. Mayflies, finger-net caddisflies, and whirligig beetles. Sideswimmers and horsetail worms labor in the shadows, unsung Good Samaritans, balancing our topsy-turvy world. Wriggling and buzzing, bubbling, and chittering, they harvest food from water, air, and soil. Then larger vertebrates—fish, frogs, birds—eat them. No macroinvertebrates, no ecosystem.

Arriving at the golf course's border with the Catkin Marsh, I pull out clippers, which I usually have on hand. Easing into a blackberry thicket, I snip a slow passage through thorny vines until I stand, bleeding but triumphant, on the cusp of new territory. Parting the dead branches of a relict apple tree, I step onto the Catkin Marsh's forest-fringed wetland meadow. Black-tailed deer, coyotes, and kestrels occupy this seasonal wetland. A happy hunting ground for carnivores and herbivores alike.

Dense populations of sword ferns, willows, and red osier dogwoods run north from here to the Elrod Canal's perimeter. During the wet season, the land floods. That's when I put on a pair of rubber waders and stand knee-deep in water, listening to the shrill chorus of Pacific tree frogs.

Close to a large industrial building, Himalayan blackberries and bull thistles *(Cirsium vulgare)* demark the western edge of the Catkin Marsh. Where I stand, deer-mashed grass gives way to a scraggle of broken bottles, cans, and cardboard. Even an old circuit breaker box. At the base of a weeping willow, I discover the remains of a tent camp. A fire pit holds a scorched sardine can, one moldy wool sock, a toothbrush, and a tattered olive-green blanket.

Further on, common teasels *(Dipsacus fullonum)* join the prickly crew of invasive plants. Like blackberries and thistles, they're often eradicated, but goldfinches like to harvest their seeds. The teasel collects rainwater in the cup-shaped cavity between its lance-like leaves and flowering stem. This often attracts flocks of thirsty bushtits *(Psaltriparus minimus)*, tiny lead-colored birds who make lovely, one-syllable chirps called a "short spit." Even hummingbirds like to take a dainty sip from a teasel. Insects often fall into these drowning pools. A bonus feeding station for birds.

A muddy track leads me north through a mixed deciduous-evergreen forest. I enter another large meadow, the Columbia River a half mile north, PDX Airport just to the east. The Bureau of Environmental Services and the Port of Portland manage this section of seasonal ponds, side channels, drainage canals, scattered stands of cottonwoods, and a dozen or so portable beehives.

A quarter mile east, I stop next to a lone beaver-felled black cottonwood. Woodchips litter the ground. The tree's a hundred yards from water. A long way for this fattywhompus to waddle just to sharpen its teeth.

On a previous trip here, I noticed two adult coyotes tailing me fifty yards back. They began to howl. Not a friendly-glad-to-see you howl. More of a get-the-hell-out-of-here howl. I walked into an adjacent forest, but they followed, still howling. I felt a little nervous. Did I look like a hamstrung doe? I saw movement next to a deadfall of birch and western red cedar. A trio of very cute coyote cubs appeared, running in circles and yipping. The two adult coyotes—likely the parents—yipped back at them. I got the memo. I was trespassing on family turf, so I prudently retreated.

Today I stumble onto another discovery. A rotting, hollowed-out red alder stump hosts a boil of bright red ladybugs (or lady-birds). A gorgeous sight. The French call them *les bêtes du bon Dieu* ("beasts of the good Lord"). Kneeling for a closer look, I hear the steady hiss, buzz, and crackle of chitinous bodies. *Ssssss- zzzzzzz-k-k-k-k-k.*

Rainclouds are gathering to the south. Finding a good spot in the grass, I stretch out flat on my back, prompting a couple of nearby horned larks to scatter. Around here, they're rare. I see only a flutter of sand-colored wings. Some yellow stripes and feathery black horns. These ground scroungers are after seeds and snails.

Next to my head, stems of sawbeak sedge anchor a milky mass of cobwebs. Spiders are versatile web artists. Other than cobwebs, they weave sheet webs, woolly webs, funnel webs, and orb webs. In Oregon, two venomous arachnids—yellow sac and black widow spiders—favor cobweb-like traps. Cabbage moths and robber flies beware.

A few inches beneath my body, a vast underworld rules, a roiling republic of red wigglers, springtails, and millipedes. They decompose leaf litter, coyote scat, eggshells. Bark chips and snakeskins. These detritovores are postmortem specialists, taking apart dead grandaddy long legs, song sparrows, and taildropper slugs. From top to bottom, it's a hungry world where everything eats and excretes ceaselessly, squaring the circle of life. Recalling Mary Oliver's poem "Sleeping in the Forest" reminds me to appreciate "the small kingdoms breathing around me."

The gathering clouds bulge and grow darker, promising what farmers call a "toad choker," but I linger, a luxurious mattress of grass cushioning my backside. The ground emits an olfactory overload of enticing, earth-infused pheromones, a musky aroma—petrichor, produced by beneficial soil bacteria—that arises from the watershed's moist meadows and woodlands.

Playing their designated roles, the slough's invisible microbial allies lurk in its sediments. Some mitigate the toxicity of PCBs, dioxins, lead, arsenic, and herbicides. Archwizards of alchemy, they try to transmute the lethality of industrial waste into drinkable water, breathable air, and healthy soil.

To placate all stakeholders, the City of Portland zones parts of the slough as Open Space while declaring others Industrial Sanctuaries. Whatever the terminology du jour, the Columbia Slough watershed provides vast acreage for small and large businesses. The slough's wildlife must shoehorn themselves into a heavy-metal world. The two legged, four-legged, multi-legged, and no-legged live cheek and haunch with the human herd. A tough and adaptable army of protozoans, gastropods, insects, arachnids, amphibians, reptiles, birds, and mammals. The slough's animal kingdom suffers heavy casualties, yet survivors somehow know how to work a system that begrudges them every cubic centimeter of space.

It's hard to comprehend the slough in its complex entirety. No part adequately describes the whole, just as a hangnail or a heart isn't the full measure of a human body. Nancy and I have biked, walked, and kayaked much of the spaghettified nineteen miles of the slough. Its main east-–west channel begins at Fairview Lake between Troutdale and Gresham, then moves along at an easy pace a mile or two south of and paralleling the Columbia River. Making its way to its terminus at Kelley Point, the slough shapeshifts from splendor to squalor, providing water for trees, wildlife, farming, and industry. Though the slough is slow business, it switches identities like a quick-change artist, then does a disappearing act into the Willamette River.

During many slough adventures, we've dodged delivery trucks, climbed over barbed-wire fences, and sidestepped yellowjacket nests. Crisscrossing the slough's wetlands and cottonwood forests, we've kicked aside syringes, beer bottles, and butane cylinders. Detoured around scrapyards, gravel pits, pumpkin patches, discarded appliances, abandoned vehicles, and makeshift meth labs. We've clawed aside invasive growths of Japanese knotweed, water hemlock, nightshade, and English ivy (the kudzu of the Pacific Northwest). Pedaled along bumpy, weed-choked bike paths that ended unexpectedly. Paddled past cattails, yellow flag irises, swollen bladderwort, and flotillas of dabbling gadwalls.

On a Peninsula Canal levee walk one summer evening, we passed a young woman practicing yoga, her body a downward dog hieroglyph of counterpoise. A half mile on, two young men set up their tripod, preparing to photograph a snowy egret that was slowly advancing toward a large black-and-yellow sheep moth atop a buckthorn branch. Where the Peninsula Canal ended at the Edgewater Golf Course, two children flew a box kite, which bobbed and swirled above the grassy meadow lined with silt fences.

Passing a tent camp close to the Oregon Food Bank, we spoke with a middle-aged man in a watch cap sweeping up garbage around his trailer.

"I try to keep things tidy," he told us with a wan smile, "but people still keep dumping their garbage here. Gives the rest of us a bad name."

Each slough exploration dished up new discoveries. We felt as if we were rummaging blindly through a box of animal crackers. Beavers and birds, oh my! And leeches, too! What would we find next? Hoping to see a pileated woodpecker, we'd spy a western red-backed salamander next to our feet, its body half buried in woody debris. Or a muskrat would pop into sight, cattail fuzz on its whiskers. Dangling legs off the dock, Nancy would spy a creeping water bug scouting the underwater murk, its raptor-like pincers clinging to an air bubble.

On hot summer days, we sat in the shade of cottonwoods. Lounging on cushy mats of deep green oxalis, we watched two coyotes work the opposite shoreline for duck eggs and nutrias. During late-summer mating season, carp thrashed around in the shallows, disturbing the blue herons and mallards. Canada geese shared downed logs companionably with cormorants and red-winged blackbirds.

Exploring the slough often left us bruised, bleeding, and disoriented. Even angry. But always, we found it a hotspot of rough magic.

Around eight miles from its source, the slough sneaks between the ever-expanding Portland International Airport and the Cascade Station Shopping Mall. Over ten thousand years ago, Ice Age megafauna such as woolly mammoths, bison, and camels may have wandered here. Now mega-churches of the global economy proliferate. Big-box stores and warehouses surround the slough. Squatting on former wetlands, these edifices leave little room for wildlife. We saw no cute critters queuing up at Ikea or Target. Just coyotes, rats, and crows checking out the dumpsters at fast-food restaurants or sampling gobble-and-go gourmet roadkill.

When Lewis and Clark explored this area, they encountered Native American villages. Now corporate storefronts, looking like modern-day Potemkin villages, border attractive landscaped avenues. At congested intersections, men and women panhandle for spare change, wagging cardboard placards at passing traffic.

We laughed at one that read: "Checks no longer accepted! Venmo only!"

No matter where we went on the slough, most parts were very noisy. The combined cacophony of the human and nonhuman worlds rarely fell silent. The northern red-legged frog could manage 60 decibels. A black-crowned night heron topped out at around 68 decibels—roughly on par with the normal range of human conversation. A Mack truck's diesel-powered growl exceeded 100 decibels. A pneumatic drill, 110 decibels. The screech of a National Guard F-15 fighter jet soared above 116 decibels. The slough was a sea-level sound chamber of little voices and big voices.

Who speaks for the slough, we wondered. Who speaks for its best interests—and our own? If we don't kill its body and spirit, the slough is a giver of life. But it doesn't just recycle water, fix nitrogen, sequester carbon, and preserve wildlife. For us, it also brings the beauty and wonder of the natural world into our lives. Beauty and wonder can't be scientifically measured or figured into the GNP, but without these intangibles, the basics of life lack deeper meaning.

It's starting to rain. Time to return home. I know the Catkin Marsh tells more stories than the BES report card reveals, yet in different ways, they both say the same thing. Spaceship Earth wears a very thin skin. Though flimsy stuff, our atmosphere of nitrogen, oxygen, and argon shelters us from the icy clutches of the void, which wants to gather us up into a death hug. Right now, we are all planetary passengers being treated to a tour of the Milky Way. We're flying along close to five-hundred-thousand mph. Whoopee! What a wild ride! But if we continue breaking the rules of conduct, we're sure to get tossed out the airlock.

5 SETTLING IN

" We abuse land because we regard it as a commodity belonging to us. When we see land as a community to which we belong, we may begin to use it with love and respect.

ALDO LEOPOLD, *A SAND COUNTY ALMANAC*

. . .

SHORTLY AFTER MOVING to the Sunderland, Bruce and I began to learn more about the history of our house and property. Albert Giese built our home in 1947–48, helped by his wife and two grade-school aged girls. The year before, he'd insured the half-acre property for $800. Mr. Giese enclosed the home on three sides with a split-cedar fence, leaving the slough side open. He built a garden shed in the south yard, and later, a greenhouse for his wife, Leona, a master gardener who was renowned for her African violets and abundant blueberry crop. On the east side, the family's view of the golf course, which had opened in 1931, was softened by a row of poplars. On the west side stretched an acre of grassy field with a red barn that sheltered horses. A half dozen modest clapboard homes, each with its own shallow well and septic tank, clustered along the short dirt road, an eighth of a mile long. Built nearly a hundred feet below Columbia Boulevard on river flood-plain, all these homes were underwater, some to their rooftops, in 1948.

Though I was sad I could never take a dip in the slough's suspect waters, I felt fortunate to own a waterfront home on a quiet street within the city. With a working well and a crumbling dock to rebuild, I dreamed of sipping cool well water on a lounge chair in the sun. Of launching my kayak into wind-ruffled waters off our dock.

That first fall, we bought bird books, a better set of binoculars, and several feeders. The red-winged blackbirds found us first, swooping in with hunched red epaulets to shoo the sparrows and starlings off the black oil sunflower seeds. As the weather chilled, smoky-headed juncos and voles arrived next to sweep the ground below the feeders.

I began to study the duck species, distinguishing first the dabblers from the divers. The dabbler wigeons and mallards thrust webbed feet into the air, tipping their beaks under water for pond grasses. Then they bounced back upright like a stoppered bottle. The divers—mostly ring-necks, goldeneyes, and mergansers— slipped under the water with barely a ripple, cleaving the surface again several feet away, like an envelope opening. I found it hard not to favor the elegant divers.

We blanketed all but a tiny patch of lawn with cardboard and layered load after load of mulch and bark chips over it. Our first spring garden popped up like fairy-tale magic. Spinach with crinkly leaves the size of serving platters. Sturdy spring onions as tall as my thigh, and soccer-ball sized cabbages that exploded through the straw.

"We're living in Findhorn," I announced in amazement, proud of our vest-pocket version of the famed Scottish eco-village. But I was blissfully unaware that plant-crunching critters just needed a full season to get our change of address.

When earlier fall sunsets emptied the golf course, we headed out like children sprung from school to walk its perimeter, slowly exploring. Just over the bridge across the Buffalo Slough, a grassy berm sloped down to the main slough channel fed by side streams and quiet pools dammed by beavers. To the east, fiery maples and yellowing birches reflected sunset colors in the clear autumn water. Rows of giant sequoias lined the fairways like silent sentinels. Behind the Oregon Food Bank, frogs sang out from a fenced-in pond of cattails, falling silent when we trudged by. Willow, alder, and cherry saplings felled by beavers crisscrossed the channels.

To the north, just beyond the meadows fringed with willows and dogwoods, we discovered the gnarled remnants of an old plum orchard, planted by Japanese and Italian farmers a hundred years ago. Above the meadow, we walked a footpath through a dense thicket of alders, maples, and cottonwoods leading to a gate onto eastern Elrod Road, now Port of Portland land. Before the expanding airport swallowed the neighborhood, a clutch of modest postwar homes once lined both sides of the street.

Our friend Mike, now in his eighties, rented one of these homes in the early 1970s. He recalls riding horses in the airport meadows with Italian friends who farmed the floodplain to grow cucumbers, dill, and garlic for Portland's premier pickle company, Steinfeld's. Now just a few relict trees and crumbling concrete pads mark the spots where these homes once perched.

Close to Elrod's abandoned asphalt, we saw a dozen active beehives.

"I hope these beauties beat a fast path to our garden," I whispered as we bent to watch them buzzing in for the day.

The golf course ended at the airport's chain-link fences, encircled by a thin moat of slack water. In the twilight, we stood under a canopy of giant sequoias and gazed across the river at the purpling ridges of Vancouver. Prop planes buzzed over the trees to land between the blue lights of the short crosswind runway.

On those first evening walks, when the deer, hawks, and coyotes were our only companions, the emptied course felt like our own nature park. But the golf course, like the rest of the slough, always jolted us from easy idylls. Mornings came early. We awoke in the dark to a rude reveille of industrial mowers whose headlights crisscrossed our kitchen windows. Loud booms, which I first thought were gunfire, erupted throughout the day.

"They're air cannons scaring the geese off the runways," said Bruce.

Our breakfast nook looked out onto the ladies' tenth hole (the outdated, gendered term for the shorter option). The men's tenth hole required a longer drive across the Buffalo Slough. One early morning we watched in dismay as greenskeepers saturated the circle of spongy grass with chemical spray, barely forty feet from our window.

When we walked over to introduce ourselves, they explained they only sprayed the greens. But we weren't reassured. Our shallow well, a mere eleven feet to the water table, provided our only source of water. We couldn't afford to irrigate a half acre with Portland's pricey Bull Run water, gravity-fed from Mount Hood's foothills. We'd need to test the well water.

That first winter, our doubts about living on the slough centered on soil, water, and noise. But when we perched on the kitchen's rough pine banquette in the low morning light to eat our oatmeal, the spicy warmth of woodsmoke and coffee driving away the chill, I felt only the deep calm of home.

6 THE SUNDERLAND—LOVE IT OR LEAVE IT

❝ **If the earth were an apartment, we wouldn't be getting our security deposit back.**

JIM SHUBERT, *ZERO TOLERANCE*

. . .

THE SUNDERLAND IS hard on our ears. During the day, we hear the roar of heavy truck traffic. A quarter-mile away, freight trains honk and screech, threading a precarious passage between Columbia and Lombard Blvds. while hauling hazardous (and flammable) materials such as crude oil, natural gas, and chlorine. Our home lies on the flight path to the airport. Commercial airliners, military jets, and small aircraft flock overhead. Engines roar and shriek, scaring the crows from the treetops. Smaller commercial and private aircraft wheeze, sputter, and backfire like Model-T Fords as they swoop down to the crosswind runway just beyond the Broadmoor's giant sequoias. We worry that one day a prop plane will stall out and plow into our house.

When I complained about the industrial noise all around, Nancy said I was overreacting.

"Just tune it out," she advised. "Don't let it get into your head."

"Don't let it get into my head? I'd have to be deaf."

"Do what I do. Wear earplugs."

The Sunderland is a rough-cut neighborhood. City living stripped to the studs. About two miles square, it has a bustling blue-collar vibe that lacks the Stumptown smugness of Portland's fussy, gentrifying neighborhoods. Here, men and women drive big trucks, operate construction equipment, repair engines, fabricate sheet metal, and pack produce in large warehouses. A bustling habitat of the proletariat class (or precariat class), this neighborhood enables hard-working stiffs to make honest, sweat-of-the-brow livings.

On the flip side of cuteness, the Sunderland boasts no boutique curio shops, yoga studios, vegan restaurants, or Sunday concerts in the park. No nannies push baby carriages down tree-lined boulevards. No cutesy corner coffee shops, though in one pink-painted hut, a barista in bikini serves java to truckers on the go. Our new neighborhood could deliver the goods for most any kind of home improvement project. If we needed turnbuckles, slide hammers, or a magnetic drill press, a business called Tacoma Screw could hook us up.

Living next to the busy Broadmoor Golf Course brought its share of new hazards. Golf balls rained down on our metal roof like meteorites, one cracking a solar panel and another denting a car door. When golfers bungled a chip shot, they often scorched the greens with a blast of industrial-strength profanity, either amusing or startling our visitors.

Despite the Sunderland's auditory assaults, we've enjoyed life next to water, a place where (when pumps haven't drained off the water) we can launch kayaks into the Buffalo Slough from our dock, portage over NE 33rd Drive to the main slough, and paddle west to Sauvie Island. If we're determined enough, we can continue a hundred miles further, to the mouth of the Columbia River at Astoria.

And in isolated spots, the slough is a showboat of serendipitous beauty. We've spent idyllic days kayaking past mergansers and western painted turtles. Drifting beneath a cottonwood canopy, the bedlam of blue heron rookeries deafening us. On one open stretch of the slough, we saw an osprey strike like the proverbial bolt of white lightning. Hitting the water with its talons, in a fraction of a second it plucked up a bluegill, enduring a G-force that would explode human eyeballs.

Settling on the slough made me more curious about the watershed that feeds it. After all, 60 percent of our bodies are made of this universal solvent. A watershed must accept, collect, and distribute whatever runoff comes its way. I knew that the slough's watershed began along northeast Portland's Alameda Ridge a couple miles south and drizzled downhill via various routes into the Columbia River floodplain.

A small neighborhood called the Dekum Triangle is part of that watershed. Its streets weren't platted on a grid. They're a Euclidean mash-up of intersections more appropriately called the "Bermuda Triangle." Our younger daughter, Miranda, and her family live close by. Getting there from our house requires crossing railroad tracks and two high-speed highways. It's hardly more than a mile away, but feels much further. On cloudy days when no sun provides a guiding compass, it's easy to get lost in the Dekum's crazy cat cityscape.

The Dekum Triangle is a diverse mix of century-old Portland bungalows, modest postwar and midcentury homes, modern infills, apartment buildings, brew pubs, and pizza joints. I took a walk there, hoping to gain insight into the nature of water flowing our way. Every street was a miscellany of well-maintained and not-so-well-maintained houses. Some homeowners had posted signs, proclaiming their backyards as certified bird habitats. Many houses had solar panels, rain barrels, hummingbird feeders, blueberry shrubs. Lots of kale and arugula gardens, too. Hybrid and all-electric cars occupied driveways. A bumper sticker on one read: "Thank you for not breeding."

Walking there one afternoon, I encountered a young man who seemed lost. Wearing only soiled underpants, he lurched barefoot down the middle of the street, slapping both sides of his head. *Whap, whap, whap, whap.* His cheeks were persimmon red. As cars swerved around him, he stopped and shouted at me: "NOT MY MONKEY! NOT MY CIRCUS!"

Walking on, I plotted my downhill route back home, imagining myself as a drop of rainwater. My soluble self goes with gravity, some of me following impervious streambeds of asphalt and concrete. Meandering through the middle reaches, I soak up the flotsam of each neighborhood. Soil. Leaves. Detergents. Paint thinners. Herbicides and synthetic fertilizers. Dog poop and truck-squashed squirrels. In a hard downpour, I ride the roadside gutters, rafting on Class VI rapids over tree litter and glass shards from clouted cars.

After that, it's a dirty dive beneath the railroad tracks and highways before coming up for air at industrial sites where I take my fill of grease, oil, metals, and microplastics. Arriving at the slough, I bear gifts from afar for fish, frogs, turtles, freshwater mussels, and birds.

The slough has good water and bad water, depending upon time, place, and who's doing the testing. Its notoriety as a dumping ground for hazardous wastes is well-deserved, yet these adulterated waters have always attracted wildlife and nature-loving humans.

Still, the industrial abuses persist, inflicting additional ecological injuries upon the slough and its biotic communities. Environmental reports make grim reading. Heavy metals like lead, arsenic, cadmium, and mercury and forever chemicals like polychlorinated biphenyls (PCBs) biomagnify up the food chain, befouling land, air, and water as they deliver bad news to plants and animals. These toxins circulate in every stream and bloodstream. They lock themselves into bones, brains, and livers.

The slough has to swallow what its watershed delivers. The slough off-gasses suspect odors, as if suffering from an upset stomach. It has its own special stink. Not the simple country stink of steaming cow pies or a dead chicken. Among its olfactory offenses, slough stink includes sharp whiffs of diesel exhaust and burning plastic. When Nancy and I pass active smokestacks, we pinch our noses, trying to shut out noxious fumes. At night, a miasma of industrial odors often wafts over the water. What are we smelling? Hydrogen sulfide? Benzene? And what about methane, which is odorless? Only a forensic chemist would know for sure.

Fear of flooding added to our other apprehensions about the slough. We were close to the Columbia River and roughly ten feet above sea level. Like history, floods always repeat themselves, changing up people, places, and dates as they hammer home the same unlearned lessons. Half a century after the Vanport Flood, the Army Corps of Engineer's levees failed during 2005's Hurricane Katrina in New Orleans, resulting in catastrophic death and widespread property damage. The Columbia River floodplain—home to the slough—features an earthen latticework of Corps-engineered levees. Could they withstand a major flood or 9.0 earthquake and hold back the river? We had our doubts.

The Sunderland was a ragbag of amazements. It had surprises for all five senses. Some good. Some bad. Hard to predict what might come tumbling out.

Nancy put our problematic neighborhood into perspective. "I know it's got its drawbacks, but this is our home now, and I love it."

I had to admit it was growing on me, too.

7 UN-NESTED

> That's what people do when they find a special place that's wild and full of life, they trample it to death.

CARL HIAASEN, *FLUSH*

. . .

A BALL OF BROWN FUR, mouse-sized, lay motionless on the concrete steps leading to the water. I bent over it, expecting a mole or vole snagged by one of the feral cats that stalk the slough banks. But a tiny skeletal wing unfolded, velvety skin stretched over matchstick bones. Then the fur ball lifted with breath. It was alive!

I called our daughter Miranda, who was sunbathing on the deck. In her senior year of high school, she was still home our first year in the house. With two cottonwood sticks, we nudged the fur ball onto its back. The sudden sight of needle-like teeth around a cherry red tongue made us both jump. It was a bat, its tiny mouth open in a silent cry of alarm.

"Is it a baby?" Miranda asked. "It's scary looking."

"I don't know. Let's flip it back over. Maybe it'll recover."

For the next half hour, we sat on the steps watching the bat and chatting about Miranda's college applications. The little mammal pulsed with quick breaths, its wing now re-tucked underneath. Then dusk fell, the air chilled, and it was time to make dinner.

"Let's move it off the pavement into the fuchsia," I said, sending her off for a garden spade. "Maybe it will be okay if nothing finds it." Fake optimism for my tenderhearted daughter. The next morning the bat was gone. Most likely eaten by a raccoon or cat—or maybe, just maybe, it flew away.

The week before, we'd leveled a death sentence on the two old cottonwoods that bent dangerously toward the house. Both had rotting cores, like many aging cottonwoods that grow near water. After the winter's heavy snow, they'd dropped large branches. Woodpeckers and squirrels had clawed holes in the crumbling cambium, and raccoons had carved out the base of the largest tree, leaving a sodden pile of reeking feces nearby. With mixed feelings, we called in an arborist.

The tree team arrived on a warm May afternoon. We moved a patio table to the strip of grass in the east yard and invited friends for a late lunch to watch the action. Forking up pasta topped by our first garden's spinach, pea shoots, and scallions, we watched with awe and anxiety as a lean young man scaled the first tree, stopping halfway up to rope up the largest branch before sawing it off and lowering it carefully to the ground team. He continued shimmying up, methodically sawing branch after branch until he closed in on the treetop, over forty feet up. Then he began topping off the trunk from there, leaning back into his harness for leverage.

Hours later, with both trees down, the crew chain sawed the trunks into dozens of thick rounds, each weighing a couple hundred pounds. They rolled them toward their pickup to haul away. Bruce flew out of his chair.

"Leave it here!" he yelled in frantic Spanglish. "*¡Por favor!*" Both arms waved toward the ground. "*Puedo usarlos!*"

I stared at him dumbly. Scores of massive cottonwood rounds tumbled together in chest-high heaps in the lower yard, an area we called The Bog for its tough cordgrass and propensity to flood in spring rains. Now The Bog was an unnavigable labyrinth of leafy main branches and sawed-up slabs. It looked like a tornado had struck.

"I've got plans for it all," Bruce assured me. "It's good biomass."

I knew little about the two species of endangered bats that roost in riparian cottonwoods and drink from the slough. One of these, the silver-haired bat, nests in bark crevices and snags. The other, the larger hoary bat, prefers tree foliage for nesting. Golf course trees near water attract these bats as they migrate to the Northwest in late spring. The bats swoop low over open water, foraging for dragonflies, mosquitoes, and other insects. Over land, they savor soft-bodied insects like the giant moths that circle our porch lights.

Once a decade, the city conducts inventories of slough wildlife. As of this writing, 2010's survey was the most recent. (COVID and late summer wildfires delayed 2020's inventory.) In 2010, the year after we felled the trees and discovered the downed bat, sightings of silver-haired and hoary bats earned the Broadmoor Golf Course a Special Habitat Area (SHA) designation.

Since then, the silver-haired bat has recovered to healthy numbers. But the hoary bat still struggles. It's the bat species most likely to be killed by wind turbines, which they mistake for trees, as they migrate. I have no idea which species our tiny fur ball was. In the years since the cottonwoods came down, we've relished the summer sight of bats circling over the water, darting back and forth through insect columns that rise after dusk. But the bats disappeared entirely in September 2020, either driven out or choked out by wildfire smoke.

Little doubt, though, that our first spring on the slough, our felling of the two cottonwoods almost certainly dislodged a bat nest and plunged a helpful insect eater to its doom. Despite our desire to host a wildlife haven on the slough, we'd already bloodied our hands. The law of unintended consequences spares no one.

8 IF NUTRIAS RULED THE WORLD

" Canned nutria is available in some deli-
catessen stores of the larger cities of the
United States as a specialty item at a very
high price.

LOUISIANA STATE UNIVERSITY
AGRICULTURE AND MECHANICAL
COLLEGE CIRCULAR, 1963

. . .

OUR FIRST SPRING in the house, Nancy and I were walking our large lab mix, Sadie, when she flushed a nutria from the slough. Trapped on an open patch of scrub grass, this semi-aquatic rodent looked like a cross between a beaver and a very fat Norway rat and seemed bulky enough to play right tackle for the NFL. It waddled in circles, searching for an escape route, its burly back matted with mud. Sadie, excited, closed in for the kill. Then suddenly, the nutria pivoted and faced its attacker.

Nancy lunged for Sadie's collar. Too late. The nutria pushed off on its hind legs, performing a balletic leap like the hippo in Walt Disney's Fantasia. Unbelievably, its twenty-plus pounds soared a full vertical foot. Sadie yelped as the nutria sank its long incisors into the bridge of her nose. I saw yellow-orange teeth. Smoker's teeth. The nutria landed on its back, righted itself, slid down a muddy bank, and disappeared into the sheltering muck of the slough.

Sadie charged after it. I called her back, but she had murder on her mind. For the next two hours, she splashed along the shore, searching for her assailant. After sunset, she finally returned home sans nutria, her coat slimed with mud and algae, her wounded nose weeping blood.

Before moving here, I'd rarely even seen a nutria. Now at dusk, I often spotted scattered colonies of them. Looking like a fleet of tugboats, their dark furry bodies navigated the slough, their round rat tails acting as rudders. Sometimes I tossed a rock at them, just to see them dive underwater with a soft, cartoon-like *kerplunk* and reappear moments later.

Nutrias are indefatigable diggers. Their tunneling severely erodes the slough bank, causing cave-ins that expose abandoned burrows and nutria nurseries. At the mouth of each tunnel, a well-worn path slants down to the water, a muddy slip'n'slide for swift escape from coyotes.

By human standards, a nutria is a hot bag of nickels. It's not river-otter cute. Or even wombat cute. Water disguises its blubbery body, but climbing onto land, the nutria forsakes all claims to adorability. It moves with the comical gait of a hipshot humpalump, chest scraping the ground. A nutria has a chunky, no-neck head, a scaly tail with sparse hairs, webbed hind feet, a whiskery snout, and thick brownish-red fur. Trying to glamorize the unglamorous, I imagined them as klutzy knockoffs of Jeremy Hillary Boob, PhD, the pear-shaped polymath professor in *Yellow Submarine*.

Nutrias may look cartoonish, but they're weapons of mass destruction. They don't just dig tunnels. Working alongside beavers and muskrats, they strip the slough clean of small trees, shrubs, and other plants. Nutrias attack at night. Ignoring the invasive plants, they gorge themselves on the top-notch stuff.

I learned this disturbing fact early on after spending two back-breaking weeks in the north yard next to the slough. Digging up well-established invasive Himalayan blackberries, bindweed, and English ivy, I replaced them with native plants: Willows, red osier dogwoods, and cattails mixed in with camas, wapato, pines, and red alder. About fifty plantings total.

The morning after I completed my project, I rose early to check on it. To my horror, all my new plants were clear-cut like an old growth forest, each shrub and tree chewed down to the roots. A telltale trail of woodchips led to the water. As I surveyed the damage, the muscles around my eyes clenched.

Viewing the mayhem, Nancy shook her head. "Our coyote friends are asleep on the job."

I bellyached to our next-door neighbor Karen about my problem. "It's like I'm operating a restaurant called McNutria's," I said. "A buncha amphibious warthogs are pigging out on the fat of our land."

She shrugged. "You could shoot them, but it's illegal to fire weapons in the city."

We both laughed. Nighttime gunshots were frequent in our neighborhood. Sometimes, the police actually arrived when called.

The nutrias might be entrenched in the slough, but I swore these tubby lumpkins weren't going to bully me into submission. Along the slough edge of our property, I built a three-foot wire fence anchored into a wall of large rocks, hoping my DIY Maginot Line would thwart any marauders with the midnight munchies. I replanted again, confident that no nutria could breach such a formidable barrier.

The next night they attacked like Panzer tanks, flattening my wire fence, rolling the rocks into the water, and shoving aside remaining obstacles. They even chewed up the wood stakes I'd pounded into the ground to thwart their advance. My Maginot Line was more like a munch-and-go line. Willows and cattails vanished in the feeding frenzy.

Next, I tried a live cage trap, baiting it with apples and peanut butter. I camouflaged the trap with branches and wedged it between some logs close to the water. The following morning, I discovered a very angry raccoon trapped inside. As I approached, it growled and lunged at me. Apprehensive about coming too close, I struggled to open the cage door. With preternaturally flexible fingers, the raccoon tried grabbing my hand and pulling it through the cage toward its bared fangs. Finally, I used a shovel handle to lift the latch. The raccoon sauntered out and scaled a cedar. Halfway up, it turned and shot me a withering look of contempt. Then it disappeared into the canopy.

Undaunted, I boned up on nutria knowledge. Know your enemy, and all that. Its genus name, Myocastor, comes from ancient Greek for "mouse or rat beaver." Laughably, in Spanish nutria means "otter." In Brazil, the nutria is called ratão-do-banhado, which translates as "big swamp rat," but throughout Latin America, they're commonly called coypu. To me, they were just ersatz beavers with rat tails.

Female nutrias are perpetual birth machines. They can reproduce at four months, sometimes pumping out three litters a year. One litter may have thirty to forty offspring. Very bad news. Even worse, nutria feces contaminate drinking water with liver flukes and tapeworms. Nutrias can get and transmit rabies. Luckily, Sadie was up to date on her shots.

The nutria's spoor print traces back to 1889. That's when US entrepreneurs imported thousands of nutrias to California from South America, planning to use them for food and fur coats. This venture tanked. Grilled nutria sliders with a side of crispy fries didn't make it onto many menus, and the wealthy didn't show much desire to warm their necks with the pelts of mangy swamp rats.

Federal and state agencies eventually rebranded nutrias as "weed cutters," hoping they might eradicate vegetation that choked off boat traffic or blocked storm drains. With much fanfare, these furry foreigners were introduced in Oregon in the 1930s, to farm for fur and for weed control. But a decade later, noxious weeds still ruled the waterways. Seems nutrias are food snobs, preferring Sitka willows to Japanese knotweed and water hemlock.

Thousands of liberated nutrias soon multiplied in watery rural, suburban, and urban settings, creating environmental havoc. In the Columbia Slough, the nutrias have built an invincible empire.

Maybe we should heed Louisiana's lead. Nutrias infest the Bayou State, but officials there pay out a six-buck bounty for each confirmed kill. A cut-off tail is proof of the deed.

A Louisiana company called Marsh Dog briefly marketed nutria for pet snacks before the COVID-19 pandemic sabotaged their business model.

Another Louisiana company—Righteous Furs—has a catchy slogan: "Save our wetlands: Wear more nutria." They call nutrias "beavers with a Cajun accent." Guilt-free furs for those who enjoy wearing dead animals.

New Orleans culinary heavyweight Paul Prudhomme once served nutria as a unique amuse-bouche. Perhaps he paired sassafras root beer and swamp cabbage with rodent schnitzel.

Closer to home, a chef named Dave Budeau from Corvallis, Oregon, won the 2012 Invasive Species Cook-Off. The event's motto was "Mastication is Eradication!" Budeau's award-winning recipe was pulled smoked nutria.

Apparently, nutria bile is a craze in South Korea, where it is even more valuable than a bear's. Containing a compound called ursodeoxycholic acid (UDCA), it helps treat liver ailments. South Korean food critic Hwang Kyo-ik argues that nutrias belong on the family dinner table. "Meat is delicious," he reports. "The color is light pink and similar to that of pork. Marbling is fine and dense. The flavor is very light, and texture is very tender."

And yet not many people want nutria on the family dinner table. If we don't eat them or wear them, what can we do with them? We can't ignore them. They multiply at will, overwhelming waterways and devouring beneficial plants, shrubs, and small trees.

Like any wild animal, nutrias just won't conform to human expectations. The Pandora's box of the natural world is full of poppies, bumblebees, and birds. River otters and tree frogs. Deer ticks, leeches, tapeworms, hornets—and nutrias. Whether *E. coli* or blue whales, everybody's gotta eat. Left unmolested, Mother Nature sorts out producers from consumers, imposing checks and balances on any creature trying to climb too high on the ladder of life.

Paul Hawken, the environmental activist, writes "Biological diversity is messy. "It walks, its crawls, it swims, it swoops, it buzzes."

Myocastor coypus mostly digs, chews and swallows. Wherever it goes, it leaves a huge mess behind. Like most invasives, it's the enemy of biodiversity.

9 HOUSE AND SKY

> I alternate between thinking of the planet as home—dear and familiar stone hearth and garden—and as a hard land of exile in which we are all sojourners.

ANNIE DILLARD, *TEACHING A STONE TO TALK: EXPEDITIONS AND ENCOUNTERS*

. . .

Mr. Giese, as he was known in the neighborhood, built a solid home, but his design sense was puzzling. The small galley kitchen with its hand-hewn cabinets and plank pine banquette was walled off from the dining room. And the tiny dining room, barely wide enough to allow us to push chairs back from the table, was boxed in by a half-glassed inner hallway that led to a bedroom. On the other side of the hallway was the living room. The entire one-story house, 1,900 square feet, was only two rooms wide. Three inner pine-paneled walls left it dark and claustrophobic.

Jeremy, Bruce's adult son, toured the premises.

"What do you think?" I asked.

He took a few moments to answer, his wide hazel eyes roving the cramped spaces. "Is this what you meant when you said you wanted to move to the country?"

Shortly after moving in, we invited over an architect we'd worked with previously to help us think about the space. Keyan walked the perimeter of the house first, then went inside and bent to peer out a creaky double-hung window that faced east. Its rope pull was frayed.

"This house needs more glass," he said. "These views are your artwork."

Keyan's design would bring the outside in by adding more glass and removing all three inner walls. To support the roof, Dale, our general contractor, friend (and also my ex-husband), came up with a creative solution. He "sistered-in" a large beam anchored to the attic floor at forty-five degrees. After that, swapping out a bedroom with the living room connected living room and dining room in an open flow along the east side.

New floor-to-ceiling glass panels brought in the water view to the north. And a bank of four four-foot wooden casement windows opened to the long rolling green fairways dotted with black locusts, willows, cedars, and sequoias to the east. Also, Dale repurposed the knotty pine from removed inner walls to build new moldings, cabinets, and an inset bookcase in the living room where a bedroom closet had been.

"This place is mesmerizing," said Dale, staring out the window as he packed up his tools late one afternoon. "The birds are a major distraction. Good thing I'm not charging by the hour."

We agreed. Like most remodels, this one took longer than planned. Cutting new windows and doors through half logs was no child's play. For five months, Bruce and I lived life in our bedroom, relishing the nightly happy hour that soon became mandatory for our equanimity. Dale and his crew worked late. Delayed in prepping dinner after getting home from work, I poured wine instead and retreated to our bedroom with a plate of cheese and crackers, settling into an easy chair turned toward the slough view. In three months, I put on fifteen pounds.

When the work was complete, warm pecan floors glowed and pinewood framed expanses of new casement windows that opened to nature. A small soapstone woodstove heated the main rooms. Visitors were drawn to the windows like a charm of hummingbirds to a feeder. On cue, Gus the heron would lift heavy wings from the water and fly over with a squawk. "My god, he looks like a pterodactyl!" one friend exclaimed.

I wondered what Mr. and Mrs. Giese would have felt about these changes. These days, a view and open floor plan increase home values. In my grandmother's time, windows were small and leaky. She closed off back rooms in her two-story clapboard house to conserve heat. Her kitchen originally sat at the end of a screened-in porch to minimize fire risk. When feather plucking and bloodletting were staples of dinner prep, cooking was not the spectator sport it is now.

These generational changes first struck me on a road trip one summer to eastern Oregon. Bruce and I pedaled bikes up a steep hill above the small town of Pendleton. Stopping to take in a sweeping view of the basin below, we looked down on a cluster of rooftops, schools, and businesses hugging the curve of the Umatilla River. Turning around, I peered at the older homes on the street above us, a row of four-squares and two-story Victorians. On most, a single double-hung window looked down on the scenic valley below. A few homes faced uphill with no windows at all trained on the river and slope.

"Odd that they wouldn't have wanted to gaze down on this beauty," I mused.

"Winters are brutal here," said Bruce. "Staying warm was more important than a view."

Maybe the Gieses didn't need a water view. They barbecued near the slough. They lounged on the dock. They boated on and splashed in the water throughout the summer.

After the remodel, I sat on our blue corduroy sofa and gazed through sparkling glass at the northern and eastern corners of our property. I could now spy the bald eagle moving off the cottonwood snag and heading northwest. In two breaths, it would cross into view through the glass doors and alight on one of the four Douglas firs rimming the men's tenth green. This was its favorite spot for observing ducklings paddling in low water. A raptor of routine, that one.

I was delighted with our new windows. Windows concerned me little in our previous home. I'm embarrassed to admit I never stepped outside to wash a single one. Inside, I Windexed maybe a handful of times in the nearly twenty years we lived there.

Like many older Portland bungalows, the deep eaves and exposed rafters of our former home blocked light, keeping the hundred-year-old house cooler through summer but obscuring accumulating grime. Many windows were painted shut entirely. The few that did open had rusty, brittle screens. We lived those years behind closed blinds, busy with work and child-rearing.

Now my gratitude for glass shows up in a twice-yearly ritual of window washing, inside and out. First in late spring before popping in the screens and throwing open the casement windows to fresh air. And again in the fall, when we build our first fire and I remove the screens, hauling them up to the attic to overwinter after vacuuming out mats of cottonwood seeds.

One Sunday morning was a perfect late fall day for window washing, crisp, with highs predicted in the mid-fifties. I popped up from a half-read Sunday paper to gather my gear: a belt with pouches to hold a squeegee, a sponge, hand broom, and spray bottle of white vinegar water. I lifted out the screens so that clean, bare windows would sharpen the winter views. Towel over shoulder, step stool in hand, I moved outside to find dozens of spider webs glistening in the morning light, their powdery egg sacs tucked into the window corners with sun-dried crud. Using the hand broom, I swept off the spiders sans apology.

"Shoo!" I said. "Spin your webs somewhere else."

A low fog lingered between the hillocks of the golf course, and frost whiskered the greens. The Canada geese were landing, taking off, and landing again in hordes, spiraling and honking their mysterious bugles and alarms. At this migration time, the geese appeared disoriented and agitated. Some constellated into perfect skeins at take-off. Others scattered, spinning off stragglers who honked mournfully as they crisscrossed the sky, hunting for their tribe.

Moving down the east side of the house, I sprayed each window with vinegar water, scrubbed with the rough side of the sponge, and squeegeed in overlapping swaths, blotting liquid at the sill with the dry cloth on my shoulder. At the twelfth window—the last one—I paused to admire the reflection of geese off clean glass. Hundreds hovered over the greens, landed, squawked, and took off again.

My forearms prickled in the warming sun. If I stayed out much longer, I'd need to shed the wool sweater. The homey smell of fried onions and hash browns signaled our neighbors making breakfast before piling into their car for church. I gave a nod to the geese, my own Sunday choir, and headed inside.

As Keyan had envisioned, the twelve new windows and four glass panels relegated our tattered art prints to the giveaway pile. Now I can pinpoint exactly where the sun rises during each season. In summer, it illuminates the red cedar trunks rooted in the slough to the northeast. At the fall and spring equinoxes, it rises directly out my kitchen window, seeming to torch the north side of Mount Hood. The pale winter sun lifts above a row of silver maples that line the hill south toward Columbia Blvd.

On clear nights, I go outside to check for moonrise. October 13, 2019, I caught the full hunter's moon, named for the time of year to lay in meat and other stores for winter. The hunter's moon recharges our spirits, energizing us to face the darker months to come. This one rose just after sunset, a fat orange ball set against a purpling eastern sky. At three a.m., I awoke in our bedroom to a silver stream of moonlight flowing over our dark red comforter. Just before sunrise, the hunter's moon set, an alabaster disk cradled between the neighbor's firs.

10 MOTHER OF STARS

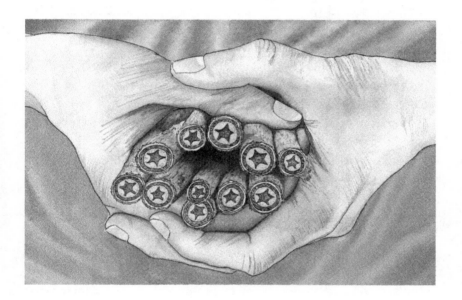

❝ **Perhaps you have noticed that even in the very lightest breeze you can hear the voice of the cottonwood tree**

BLACK ELK, "SONG TO WAKAN TANKA"

. . .

COTTONWOODS MAKE the enemies list of homeowners, who call them "trash trees," "hazard trees," and "widow makers." Their leafy branches act as giant parasols, throwing deep shade on gardens. In a storm, cottonwoods topple over and pancake houses. Their trunks rot and collapse without warning. Sometimes they kill people.

By our second year on the slough, I'd had it with the black cottonwoods just outside our yard. All three of them. They crowded together closely enough to pass for Siamese triplets. Cottonwood crud was everywhere. Leaves, branches, bark. These trees were falling apart like a cheap suit. In the mornings, they shaded our property, making it difficult to grow vegetables. Our tomatoes and peppers were starved for sunlight. I didn't want to cut the trees down. Just to top them off. Maybe twenty or thirty feet, leaving the snags for animal habitat.

Taking matters into my own hands, I scaled one cottonwood so I could prune enough branches to admit sufficient light.

Nancy stood below, frowning. "You're gonna kill yourself. We should've hired a professional."

"Too expensive." An arborist had bid $5,000 to do the job.

Together, two of the trees formed a V-shape, so I nailed between their trunks a succession of two-by-four ladder rungs. Then I climbed, hammered, and sawed. Branches crashed down into the understory. About twenty feet up, the trunks diverged far enough that I had to switch my technique, nailing each new rung to the larger, sturdier trunk. Up I went, fighting off vertigo.

Approaching the topmost branches, I felt the wind. The cottonwoods swayed. Limbs creaked. Leaves shimmered. I passed an abandoned squirrel's nest. All around me, birds moved through the branches. Crows, robins, red-winged blackbirds. On a side branch, a downy woodpecker twisted around and eyed me, the red patch on its head catching a spot of sunlight.

"That's high enough," Nancy shouted. "Climb down. Now!"

Returning to earth without breaking my neck, I thought dark thoughts about cottonwoods. What good are they? If I could understand their creaky utterances, I might hear them asking me the same question. *Humans. What good are they?*

In "Don't Fence Me In," Cole Porter crooned about "the murmur of the cottonwood trees." Our own cottonwoods aren't fenced in, and they murmur only when it suits them. If cottonwoods want to get our attention, they sing their leafy lungs out in a long-winded aria. In winter storms, they let loose a full-blown death wail. They shake, crack, and snap. Limbs fly down like javelins. Out in the open, I'm terrified they'll impale me.

On blustery days, the cottonwoods overshadowing our property pull rock-a-bye baby lullabies from the wind. "And down will come baby/Cradle and all." Like sails set to prevailing westerlies, heart-shaped leaves flutter softly, showing their pale underbellies. The trunks groan, branches rattle, the cottonwoods sigh. *Oh-so-slow-oh-so-slow.* Then a steady *S-h-h-h-h-h-h,* like a mother soothing her child.

On calmer days, the cottonwoods whisper sweet nothings. In the treetops, the wind's invisible fingers strum a sleepy susurrus that riffles up the scum on the slough. The birds grow quiet. Even the ducks stop dabbling. The world dozes off as cottonwood notes climb the chromatic scale, changing in pitch and duration as they usher in a suspended state of animation. Like stream debris snagged by a downed branch, time slows, comes to a momentary halt, then frees itself and moves on.

Living next to the slough, Nancy and I quickly learned that cottonwoods aren't good neighbors. They were born to occupy the open prairie beneath the wide blue sky, nobody else around except jackrabbits, antelopes, coyotes, and a lone cowboy with his guitar. Cottonwoods never stay in their lane. In spring and fall, they're godawful litterbugs, depending upon others to pick up after them.

Cottonwoods dominate most every furlong of the Columbia Slough. They colonize canals, culverts, drainage ditches, sidewalks, and vacant parking lots. According to the experts, the black cottonwood *(Populus trichocarpa)* is a water hog, glugging down up to two hundred gallons daily. Enough to drink a small river dry. This western cousin of the eastern cottonwood *(P. deltoides)* stores water during the rainy season and releases it in times of drought. A mature tree carries over two tons of what's called "green weight." Much of this poundage is water.

Cottonwood makes good kindling, but burning a cord of it won't chase the winter chill from your bones. The tree's porous, low-density wood is classified as a hardwood. Balsa wood is also a hardwood. A real brain-twister, but both trees are angiosperms and producing seed-bearing flowers somehow qualifies them for that description. The cone-bearing gymnosperms—like pines and spruces—are softwoods. Very confusing terminology. Cottonwood pulp produces reams of flimsy printing paper. Pines and spruces, non-flimsy crossbeams. Hardwood? Softwood? Go figure.

Like hyperactive kids, cottonwoods never stay still. They're always up to something. In spring, we admire their glossy, tough leaves. Then come multitudes of sticky male-female capsulated seeds called catkins, a fuzzy, necklace-shaped fruit. Cottonwoods are dioecious: Male trees produce pollen, while female trees release a storm of "cottonwood snow." Floating everywhere, this fluffy stuff lays down a suffocating blanket of misery that gunks up gutters, vents, window screens, and nostrils. Spiderwebs and flowers disappear beneath the deep drifts that look like snow. Allergies flare up. Cottonwood snow won't rake easily. Better to vacuum it up or spray it down and scrape it away.

Nancy pulled apart the cotton candy wrapping of a catkin, plucked out tiny green seeds, and ate a few.

"It's like fairy floss with nuts," she said. "No wonder the birds go crazy for it."

I tried some. They tasted like peppery sesame seeds.

Ecologists consider cottonwoods beneficial. These trees preserve watersheds and wildlife. They stabilize crumbling stream banks and make effective windrows and flood buffers. They feed and shelter wildlife, providing high-rise hidey-holes for fungi, bacteria, beetles, birds, and bats. Raccoons hibernate inside the trunks. The western tiger swallowtail and Persius duskywing butterflies collect cottonwood pollen. If the cottonwood hired a PR flack to tout its unsung virtues, its seedy reputation might improve.

The cottonwoods crowding our property poach resources like sneak thieves. Thick yellow roots slither in all directions. They will pirate water and nutrients and invade septic tanks and sewer lines in the same way bamboo rhizomes devastate human infrastructure.

I chop out roots and shoots, but more cottonwoods quickly sprout elsewhere.

Hugging the slough, juvenile cottonwoods grow Jack-in-the-Beanstalk fast. Over six feet a year. Some can survive two hundred years. Favorable conditions may allow a few leafy Methuselahs to age out at four centuries, but the ones growing across the slough from our house aren't so fortunate. They grow fast and die faster. Beavers bring them down with regularity.

Diseases and contaminated soil defoliate some nearby cottonwoods. Green leaves canker and drop. Plates of bark separate from the trunks. Within a few months, the trees rot in place. Industrial toxins? Root fungus? Nobody knows for sure, but something sucks the life out of them. A cottonwood cemetery of skeletal snags borders the slough. Scallops of shelf fungus appear. Woodpeckers honeycomb the trunks. Raptors and crows roost on the snags. The trees fall apart limb by limb before crashing into a bier of blackberries. Then green shoots appear. Every bone orchard soon becomes a nursery. The living rise from the dead.

Many artists have immortalized cottonwoods in songs, poems, books, photographs, paintings, and movies. The tree's wind-tortured branches offer semaphores of stoic suffering, of perseverance and tragic beauty. Even transcendence. Georgia O'Keefe painted cottonwoods in New Mexico, Maynard Dixon in Utah. Ansel Adams photographed dead cottonwoods in California's Yosemite Valley. In artists' hands, the ravaged remains of a cottonwood express sweeping statements on the human condition.

For city dwellers, cottonwoods are just a huge pain in the ass. They suck up too much water, drop trash everywhere, and clobber people's heads. In Latin, *populus* means "people," *trichocarpa*, "hairy fruited." I fear black cottonwoods and their hairy fruit form an expansionist tree tribe bent upon world domination. *Populus trichocarpa* uber alles.

Why shouldn't I just chop them all down? Here's why. Cottonwoods don't just furnish the natural world with food and shelter, and prevent erosion and droughts. They also heal physical or emotional wounds, providing naturopathic cures for whatever ails us.

The Balm of Gilead is one example. Produced from shaved beeswax and the sticky sap of the cottonwood's swollen buds, this redolent salve contains methyl salicylate, a pain-relieving compound. Cottonwood salve effectively treats burns, bruises, and scrapes. Psoriasis and eczema, too. Its pleasing fragrance—known as the "scent of heaven"—wicks away stress.

Call it cottonwood clever. First this tree violates our peace of mind, even threatening us at times with violence and sudden death. Then it offers cures to relieve our stress and pain. It's how it makes aromatic amends for trespassing into our lives.

The Mother of Stars. This is the name some Native Americans gave the cottonwood. They believed each tree gave birth to a new generation of stars. Snap a branch and in its pith you'll usually discover a five-pointed star embedded in the darker heartwood.

Nancy tried this. It took some practice, but she found the promised image. Tiny stars. From them, great cottonwoods will grow. Who's to say that cosmic dust isn't cottonwood fluff? Singing with the wind, the Mother of Stars flings her star children across the universe.

11 PULLING THE PLUG

" Nature does not hurry, yet everything is accomplished.

LAO TZU

. . .

THE YEAR after we moved in, the two sisters who helped their father build our house knocked on our door. Gretchen and Linda, then in their seventies, had learned the house had new owners. They sat at our dining room table, spry and chatty, cradling cups of coffee and talking over each other for a couple of hours, sharing lively stories from their childhoods. Both now lived on acreage outside of Portland. They'd brought a folder of photos and clippings to leave with us. Snapshots depicted them as schoolgirls post–World War II, washing their hair in an outside basin during house construction, selling lemonade for five cents from a stand, quaffing drinks above their parents' open liquor cabinet. "What, at it again?" that shot was captioned.

By the time of their visit, we'd either remodeled or reconciled ourselves to many of the home's eccentricities. One oddity that still confounded us was the second bathroom, with a two-foot-wide concrete shower stall that was too tiny to turn around in. The one time I'd showered there my butt stuck to the wet curtain.

"That was Daddy's bathroom," Gretchen explained. "He was short and skinny. No one else used it."

A few years after the house was built, Mr. Giese hauled in fill dirt to extend a lower yard eight concrete steps down toward the slough. One photo shows him thigh deep in slough water, building a retaining wall from scrap concrete. Other snapshots captured the family splashing in the water next to a rowboat. In one, Gretchen and Linda float in inner tubes and smile at the camera. In another, Mr. Giese wades hip deep with a live yellow duckling perched on his bare shoulder.

The family called the slough "the pond" and launched two boats on it every summer. Near their dock, Mr. Giese built a wooden, dirt-floored changing house, with MEN and WOMEN signs posted above green corrugated plastic privacy windows at each end. Their changing house remains in The Bog, now engulfed by the spreading aspens, willows and maples Bruce planted. Boards have popped out, and soon the structure will collapse.

"Weren't you worried about the sediments?" I asked Linda. Their slough swimming shocked me.

"Not really. Back then we didn't know about the pollution."

But her sister recalled one summer when their mother, Leona, warned them to stay out of the water. An iridescent slick had spread from the north slope, nearly reaching the Gieses' dock. Leona complained to her daughters about the farmer who owned the dairy between the Buffalo and main sloughs. He'd buried old fuel cans, she said, along with concrete and farm wastes, adding fill dirt to extend his land over the water. Common practice, apparently, at that time.

"Heaven knows what was in those leaky, rusty cans!" said Gretchen.

I had trouble squaring the sisters' idyllic-sounding 1950s childhoods with what I was learning about the slough. The golf course had opened less than twenty years before they arrived. The girls made sandwiches to sell to postwar golfers, with a side of scavenged balls, for fifty cents. They rode horses boarded in the red barn, now a rental home, three doors down. And they swam in the "pond" with friends while their parents hosted rollicking parties around a brick outdoor fireplace Mr. Giese built. These barbecues were legendary in the neighborhood, they said, their voices bright with happy memories. Leona served vodka cocktails from giant Mason jars stuffed with blueberries harvested from her twenty bushes. In one enlarged color photo, their father serves burgers off the fire to a crowd of revelers, the women in jaunty pastel push-ups and white tennies, the men in Hawaiian shirts with open necks. Fun times on the slough.

The Buffalo Slough ran deeper then, as it did our early years living here. Back then, we could easily launch kayaks from our dock, but we could not paddle far. To the east, the Buffalo dead-ended a half mile away. To the west, the culvert that discharged Buffalo Slough under NE 33rd Drive was an ancient metal drainage pipe, and only a couple of feet wide. It clogged often with fallen cottonwood branches, logs, and other debris. There was no paddling through the old culvert to meet up with the main slough and continue downstream.

To kayak to Kelley Point, where the slough spills out into the Willamette River, we had to portage boats over 33rd Drive and enter the water from the Elrod launch at the Multnomah County Drainage District. With friends, we kayaked these nine miles twice, detouring into the shallow pools at Smith and Bybee Lakes before pulling out on a muddy slope at Kelley Point for beers and snacks. Both times, the one-way trip took over three hours.

The outdated culvert under NE 33rd acted like a bathtub plug, trapping deeper water in the Buffalo Slough. Now I understood why the sisters' snapshots were ink-captioned "pond" or "lakeside." At times of heavy rain, we watched the plugged-up Buffalo overwhelm the drainage district pumps. High spring water sometimes breached our dock and flooded The Bog, even lapping the concrete steps that led up to our home, eight feet higher.

After we took down the two cottonwoods nearest the house, Bruce hired a couple of former students to help him roll and anchor the massive trunk rounds throughout The Bog. These stubby cylinders would cradle soil and provide structure for new planting areas. One day, high spring water flooded The Bog and lifted the heavy rounds, which floated quickly toward the swollen slough. Astonished at how fast a few inches of water could counter massive weight, we sped down the steps, using hands, feet, and lake rakes to herd them back. Afterward, we limped up the steps to dry land, our ankles cold, soaked, and scraped. Applying Band-Aids, I felt new respect for the power of moving water.

In those early years, the deeper, stiller water brought occasional flooding and nourished thick mats of algae in warm months. By late summer, the algae choked the water's surface. Geese, ducks, and mating carp churned narrow tracks through the green carpet. Before a party one September, Bruce and I decided to try to rake out the algae, which stank and swarmed with flying insects.

"I can spread it over the garden," Bruce said. "It'll make good fertilizer." My resourceful husband finding use for even a reeking mat of algae.

We hauled our lake rakes down to the dock and angled them out over the water. But the rakes were unwieldy, and we struggled to maintain our balance. The tines barely dented the tough mat. So I launched my kayak and set off into the muck, using a paddle to heave up and layer the thick ropes of algae back and forth over my prow. This technique proved successful. The power of my biceps to pack the prow with layer after layer of algae felt awesome. But my satisfaction soon turned to alarm as the heavy algae dragged the boat's nose down into the water. My heart raced at the prospect of tipping over and landing calf-deep in toxic sediments. I gave up, exhausted and panting.

The hole I'd managed to open in the algae was barely the size of a kitchen table. Bruce brought down a wheelbarrow, loaded a cartful of algae off the dock and spread it around new flower beds he had planted along the golf course. Within a week, the rotting algae had killed every plant, sealing rows of desiccated stems and flowers beneath a stinking sarcophagus of eukaryotic die-off.

Soon after, a flyer in the mail announced the city's plan to punch a larger, open culvert under NE 33rd Drive. The new culvert promised improved water flow and healthier fish habitat in the Buffalo Slough. We were thrilled.

"Soon we'll be able to kayak from our dock to the sea!" I bragged to anyone in earshot.

The plan depicted a large opening leading west to the main slough, with a wildlife shelf installed along the new culvert for migrating critters. I was dubious about the need for that addition since I couldn't picture any slough animal that didn't fly or swim. Even raccoons, coyotes, and rabbits go into water.

Like most public construction projects, this one proceeded in fits and starts over the next few years. When the culvert finally opened in the spring of 2014, we saw that a bioswale and boat launch had been added, with Oregon grape and other native vegetation planted on top.

On a warm, late spring day, I launched my kayak from our dock and headed west for the first time through the new culvert. I smiled at the metal wildlife shelf attached to the tunnel wall, still wondering what might take that route. Perhaps a feral cat prowling the slough? After merging with the main slough, I turned east toward Whitaker Ponds.

By that summer, though, the water in the Buffalo had drained to mere inches. Launching a kayak from the dock was impossible. Many days, it was landlocked entirely, leaving Mr. Giese's concrete wall exposed and bleached white. I sat on the deck chair and watched water striders dance over the mudflats. Why were the pumps still operating? The rains had slackened, and the Columbia River was low. The drainage district's core mission is to prevent floods by pumping water west via twelve pump stations along the slough. But this was midsummer, the months of no-rain Portland, and opportunistic plants were already springing out of the Buffalo's sediments.

We contacted Josh McNamee, an employee of the drainage district, who assured us that pumping wasn't to blame. Automatic timers were set to pump when water levels rose above three feet on measuring sticks placed at center spots along the slough.

"Pumping uses a lot of electricity," McNamee said. "We only do it when we need to."

Not satisfied, we emailed mudflat photos to the city's Bureau of Environmental Services (BES) with an invite to come see for themselves. Days later, we stood on the dock with Susan Barthel, Columbia Slough Program Coordinator. I pointed to the old, moss-covered waterline along the wall, topped by two feet of bleached concrete. Proof of ongoing low water.

"What you're seeing is natural water level variation," she explained. "The widened culvert lets the water flow more freely."

Buffalo Slough by nature was wider and shallower than the main slough, she said. This made sense but raised more questions. What about the fish and water quality in such a warm, shallow soup?

"Actually, the water quality is improving," Barthel told us. "It seems counterintuitive, but when water levels fall, more fresh water is pulled into the slough by osmosis from natural springs along the banks. The water flows faster and contains more oxygen. Eventually this means better fish habitat."

After she left, we still felt deflated. "At this rate, Buffalo Slough will dry up," groused Bruce. "Maybe eutrophication is their real plan."

We wondered whether the river otters approved of the Buffalo's fluctuating water levels. And what about the waterfowl? Lower water exposes shore nests to easy predation.

Every summer since the culvert replacement, the Buffalo has settled into a similar pattern. If rainy seasons raise the water level a few feet, the pumps kick in and drain it down. Below our dock, it never rises above a couple feet. Jumping down into a kayak is tricky.

In the summer, the shores are either mudflats, or a couple of inches lap our dock. The giant carp have mostly disappeared. Bruce says there are fewer ducks, but I'm not sure about that. I still spot rafts of them intermingling with the Canada geese every day. The nutrias and beavers still persist, carving destructive mudslides up the slope.

Unfortunately, the new native plantings at the mouth of the culvert soon vanished into thickets of invasive Himalayan blackberries and English ivy, teasels, and thistles. No maintenance workers arrived to maintain the original plantings. The NE 33rd Drive access for kayakers was gated off and abandoned.

On October 21, 2019, I spotted the first otters we'd seen since the culvert was widened five years earlier. It was early morning, and I was still in my red robe, when I noticed higher water from recent rains. Cradling a mug of coffee, I shuffled down to the dock in sandals. An adult otter stretched over a log twenty feet off the dock. She appeared to be munching a bright red crayfish. Two juveniles dove and surfaced around her. For several minutes, I watched the three of them fish, each pulling up and crunching on a red catch tangled with loose reeds. The two pups swam close to the dock, flipped onto their backs, and stared at me.

"Hi, sweethearts," I cooed. "Welcome back." Finally, the three moved east, threading in and out of the water with barely a ripple. I'd forgotten how fast otters swim.

By the next day, the water had drained to a few inches deep and the otters were gone.

At a cost of over $5 million, BES had commissioned the Army Corps of Engineers to replace the ancient culvert, with the goal to improve water quality and fish habitat. The bathtub plug was pulled, and the pumps drain water more efficiently. But the water never reaches a level that even warrants pumping. It's never breached the dock again, which stands high and dry above the mud.

Like most things about the slough, the gains and losses are so tightly intertwined they defy separation. Lower water levels bring fresher water, but for how long? If the Buffalo Slough dries to a seasonal wetland, more likely as the climate warms, it will fill with cattails, sedges, willows, and invasive plants. The pond where the Giese girls once floated their boats and swam with their friends, gone forever.

In one photo the sisters left, they are smiling teenagers with curly 1950s bobs, floating in and around a drift boat with their father and two other girls. We inherited this boat, left on the property with an old wooden oar. Bruce drilled holes in the boat, dragged it from The Bog to the south yard and planted sword ferns, redwood sorrel, and a dogwood tree in it. He propped the wooden oar close by.

When Bruce's daughter, Willow, and her husband, Eric, moved to the coast, we gave them our kayaks. I hadn't launched mine from the dock since that first heady spring when the new culvert opened. In warm, inviting weather, the water's too shallow. During the rare times when there's more water, it's usually cold and rainy. But the water that remains in the summer does seem fresher, less murky. Perhaps it's clear because there's less of it. The thick algae mats of late summer have not returned. Instead, a skim of lacy duckweed grows in summer and lingers into fall. Mudflats are common, exposing golf balls, a washtub, and an old, cast-iron water heater. Standing on the dock, we see the criss-cross hieroglyphics of raccoon and nutria tracks.

If the Buffalo dries up entirely, I've got a plan. I'll pull on hip boots and hop off the dock. I'll slog north through the vegetation and over the berm to the main slough. Among the trees, I'll rest by the water and search for the otters.

12 FOOLS ON FIRE

66 **All truly great thoughts are conceived by walking.**

FRIEDRICH NIETZSCHE, *TWILIGHT OF THE IDOLS*

. . .

I'M off on another neighborhood walk, trying to air out my anger. Just watched a scroungy gray cat slink through my yard, its jaws clamped down on a large northern flicker *(Colaptes auratus)*. I gave chase but the damned cat escaped with its prize. The northern flicker is one of the few woodpeckers that migrate. Some call it a "harry-wicket," a name that mimics one of its calls.

As I walk the Sunderland neighborhood, the woodpecker's murder puts me in a foul mood. Stressing about bird killers diverts my attention from the traffic. The Sunderland is not pedestrian-friendly. I need to stay alert—and ready to dive for cover.

Flickers are gorgeous. They have showy white rumps, and their wing and breast feathers are a mesmerizing ripple of spots, bars, and crescents. Males flaunt their red-streaked cheeks. I watch them pecking rotten logs, their two-inch tongues lapping up carpenter ants. During mating season, they rattle the timbers of our house, beating out a four-on-the-floor territorial groove against the metal chimney. Competing for mating privileges, males engage in a vigorous thrust-and-parry beak dance for a nearby female to evaluate their performance.

Near home, I've seen flickers attacked by ravening mobs of starlings *(Sturnus vulgaris)*. Starlings like to nest in woodpecker holes, and a screeching flock of them can easily overwhelm a solitary flicker. After one gang attack, I saw a flicker perched on a black hawthorn stump, both eyes pecked out, blood trickling from the sockets.

Like pirates, starlings plunder the wealth of the land, coming and going seasonally. But cats are year-round murderers. They devour birds, bats, butterflies, dragonflies, grasshoppers, garter snakes, field mice, and more. They're born to hunt but don't always eat their kills.

Most of our neighbors let their cats roam free. It's hard on the flickers—and a host of songbirds. They're also hard on our ears. On warm spring nights the feral cats mix it up with the domestic ones. They shriek and yowl like graveyard goblins. Cat sex with a death metal soundtrack. Litters of mewling bird killers appear two months later.

Nancy and I share blame for the uptick in bird mortality. In winter, we hang bird feeders, which attract predators. No junk food for our lizards on the wing. Our feathered friends are pampered with sunflower and nyjer seeds, peanuts, suet cakes. The bird assassins approve. Sharp-shinned hawks and stoats (short-tailed weasels) nab a few birds, but cats kill the greatest number. Mostly smaller birds, like the black-capped chickadees, sparrows, juncos, and bushtits. The American Bird Conservancy estimates that cats annually kill 2.4 billion birds worldwide.

A 2019 article in *Science* magazine estimates that the US has suffered a loss of three billion birds in the last half century. Most of these losses have come from the ranks of three families: blackbirds, finches, and sparrows.

The cats can't claim full credit for thinning out the avian ranks. Habitat loss and climate change are the real bird killers. The northern flicker is especially vulnerable. Rising temperatures wreak havoc on it, but industrial logging, shopping centers, recreational roads, and housing developments deliver a devastating knockout blow. Without open fields and healthy forests to forage in, the flickers perish. Ecologists classify these birds "keystone excavators" since they hollow out forest snags, providing shelter for other cavity nesters.

Fretting about the plight of birds, I stop walking and close my eyes. No birdsong within earshot. Not even the indignant squawk of a crow or blue jay. The roar of traffic owns the soundscape. I move on again, setting a circuitous course for the Elrod Canal.

The Sunderland is one of the city's ninety-five officially recognized neighborhoods. According to a city planning website, it ranks eighty-seventh for walkability. Too much traffic, too few services. Also, double-lane highways and railroad tracks segregate the Sunderland from other neighborhoods. On the map, it looks like a gerrymandered congressional district. Wildlife outnumbers humans here, an underrepresented constituency of insects, amphibians, reptiles, fish, birds, and mammals. Forget walkability scores. The Sunderland needs flyability, swimmability, and slitherability scores. Given all the diesel exhaust, maybe a breathability score too.

Close to NE 33rd Drive, I pass a lopsided tower of wood

pallets. Cinderblocks support a rusted-out car stripped clean of engine and tires. A dingy pink house peeks out from a blackberry patch. From the far edge of what looks like a buffalo wallow, three white crosses jut from the mud. A DIY cemetery for dogs. The occupants of the pink house run a puppy mill. Apparently, not all these penned-up pooches live to see a better day.

A leathery, chain-smoking woman living here routinely shepherds a pack of yapping rat-like terriers down the hill, but her unleashed dogs sometimes bolt onto Columbia Blvd., where they join the ever-expanding roster of roadkill.

"Nothing good ever comes out of that pink house," one of our neighbors commented. "Those people give me a reverse magnetic feeling in the stomach."

I often hear the woman loudly cursing her dogs. Each one has a name that starts with an F. It's not "Fido." These free-range mutts do their business in other people's yards. One day an irate homeowner confronted her. After cussing him out, she straight-armed him in the chest. He backpedaled into his house, slamming the door. A few months ago, she reportedly punched one of her housemates.

"They were screaming at each other in the middle of the field," a neighbor told Nancy and me. "Then she decked him out. The dude didn't get up for five minutes."

"Welcome to the Sunderland," said Nancy.

I turn north on NE 33rd Drive and trudge past the city-installed bioswale. Native sedges and grasses are overgrown with blackberries and thistles. Near the Oregon Food Bank, I see a lasagna-layer pile of rotting cardboard and cottonwood leaves. A good spring soaker might transform this moldering mass into a bed of black morel mushrooms. Overnight, their spongy heads will poke up, broadcasting the short-lived, born-again bonhomie of their kind. Then they'll droop and deliquesce into a gelatinous glob. Sic transit gloria.

I step out onto the road. Vehicles zoom past. It's the PDX Grand Prix—or perhaps a pack of gearheads laying rubber as they fishtail toward the Portland International Raceway. Hardly anyone obeys the 35 mph speed limit. Even large trucks push 50–60 mph.

Between midnight and three a.m., street racers rule the roadway. These speed freaks layer the road with Gorilla-Snot, an insider name for a compound used to protect the pavement from damage. Engines shriek. Tires squeal. Cars pop wheelies, blow rods, and spin out. A pungent fog of burning rubber and car exhaust drifts across the slough. It's the fossil fuel follies. The Portland.gov website warns: "YOU RACE! YOU LOSE!" Here we see zero evidence of any losses.

I called the Portland Bureau of Transportation (PBOT) to lobby for speed bumps and a flashing yellow light along this dangerous stretch of road.

"What can you do to slow down the speeders?" I asked the guy who took my call. "It's hard to make a safe left turn off our street. Day or night."

A week earlier a speeding car had T-boned a neighbor's vehicle as she turned left onto NE 33rd Drive. The collision sheared off the back of her pickup, hurling the cab against a tree on the opposite side of the road. Miraculously, no serious injuries. Police never arrived, but neighbors called a tow truck and redirected traffic around the wreck while an off-duty RN provided first aid to my neighbor.

The PBOT employee agreed that speeding was a problem. "We could post a right turn only sign at the end of your street. How's that sound?"

"That'd penalize the people who live here," I said. "Speeders are the problem."

"The truckers hate speed bumps. Maybe we can post another speed limit sign."

"Will that stop the dragsters?"

"Who knows? That's a police matter."

Seeing a break in the traffic, I sprint across NE 33rd Drive, then go west on NE Elrod Drive toward the Riverside Golf and Country Club. The smell of hot bacon grease and baking bread wafts from the club kitchen. A few golfers loiter next to their cars, chatting and smoking.

On my left, a row of stately century-old giant sequoias overshadows the Elrod Canal. Stopping between two of these ancient heavyweights, I peer across the murky water. A lone cormorant perches on a discarded grocery cart, drying its wings. Closer in, a nutria swims slowly around a half-submerged truck tire, its eyes squeezed shut.

A hundred yards on, a gravel pathway skirts a tent camp, then parallels the canal. A scattering of fresh woodchips lies next to toppled red alders and Oregon ashes. Beavers. They keep their choppers sharp in case the Sunderland reverts to its original wetland status, prompting a renewed demand for log dams.

I continue along the path. Invasive plants have put down deep roots here. They choke out native grasses, sedges, and reeds. Teasels, thistles, knotweed, and garlic mustard throttle the red osier dogwoods and willows. In the canal, mallards swim through thick growths of parrot feather milfoil *(Myriophyllum aquaticum)*. On the berm between the trail and road, twinberry shrubs and ponderosa saplings wear raggedy skirts of bedstraw, purple nutsedge, and leafy spurge.

Giant hogweed *(Heracleum mantegazzianum)* towers over one section of the trail. Also called the cartwheel-flower for its white umbrella-shaped flowerheads, giant hogweed has caustic sap that produces skin blisters and severe rashes.

Another intruder colonizes the canal. A tall poisonous perennial with striking purple-red berries, it's called pokeweed or polk weed. Despite their toxicity, the tapered green leaves of *Phytolacca decandra* can be boiled to make an edible spinach-like dish. Tony Joe White's 1968 hit single, "Polk Salad Annie," celebrated this plant. The song describes an impoverished Louisiana girl who has nothing but pokeweed greens to eat.

Another half mile and the trail ends. I rejoin Elrod Drive as it curves left to dead-end at the Multnomah County Drainage District, a cluster of concrete buildings enclosing a massive pump system. The drainage district's policy of down-to-the-dregs pumping prevents flooding of homes and businesses. Unfortunately, it also hampers kayaking, confounds waterfowl, and promotes the spread of invasive plants, which swiftly take advantage of new turf.

I angle left on a short trail leading to where the main Columbia and Buffalo sloughs converge at the station's ginormous pumps. A floating rake bar isolates upstream garbage. It works like logging booms that corral timber harvests. No logs here. Just a gently rocking raft of plastic bottles, trash sacks, and blocks of Styrofoam.

Here kayakers can portage a short distance around the pump station to the next leg of the slough, heading west to its mouth at Kelley Point. The payoff is a spectacular array of wildlife in water, on shoreline, and at treetop. More photo opportunities at this location than in most national parks. More solitude, too.

I return to Elrod Drive and climb the slough levee. At the top, a kayaker's pathway slants steeply down to the main channel. Directly ahead, a locked gate surrounding private land bars further foot traffic along the levee. A friend who owns a bike store once scaled the gate. Pulling his bike behind, he climbed over the cyclone fencing and began riding west along the main channel of the slough.

"All of a sudden, this crazy woman came running out of the woods," he told me. "She was screaming that I was trespassing. She had two little goats with her. They charged at me and butted my bike. I'd never seen attack goats!"

To my right, the levee over the Peninsula Drainage Canal provides a goat-free walking route, forming a graceful S curve that stretches approximately a mile north to Marine Drive. Taking it, I stop to admire the open sky and snow-clad volcanoes. Jetliners swoop low to land at the airport, turbofan engines whining. Across the Columbia River, the city of Vancouver crouches on the bluffs.

It's a warm afternoon. Below me, scores of western painted turtles, freshly emerged from the canal mud, bask in the sunshine atop dead half-submerged cottonwood logs. The State of Oregon lists this species as "sensitive-critical," but they are abundant here today. On one log, I count seventeen turtles, including hatchlings. From my vantage point on the levee, the baby turtles are the size of silver dollars, their shells brown to pale green. A blue heron wades toward the log, intending to snatch them up. I hear a rapid *kerplash, kerplash, kerplash*. Only a few large turtles remain on the logs, sharing space with several mallards.

I have a friend with a turtle obsession. Walking with me here, he's yearned to poach a few to rehome in his large nature pond, already well populated with frogs, newts, and salamanders.

"I need some turtles," he told me months ago. "I have special bait traps I can set late at night. Turtles love baloney."

"You wanna get arrested for turtle kidnapping?" our daughter asked, hearing his plans. "Pretty damn embarrassing for your wife and kids."

Properly chastised, my friend settled for admiring the turtles from a distance.

Across the canal, house roofs appear above a ridgeline of cottonwoods. Horses, cows, and sheep tread the eroded shoreline, grazing on sparse patches of grass. A man bumps along on his ATV, following a private trail that loops through the woods down to the water. A raft holding a plywood bird blind floats a few yards offshore, a rope tethering its stern to a cottonwood stump. Seeing me on the levee, the man stops his ATV and dismounts. We exchange greetings, and he shouts that he doesn't use the blind to hunt birds. He only photographs them.

Further on, the Columbia River Correctional Institution appears on the right, situated among trees and side canals. I next pass Dignity Village—an intentional tiny home community. Then the noisy Sunderland Yard Recycling Facility.

A broad meadow opens between the dike and NE 33rd Drive, a large horse barn and stable marking the southern perimeter. Dozens of dark green plastic silt fences divide the meadow into long grassy strips. A Port of Portland employee explained that these three-foot-high fences discourage Canada geese from taking flight above the runway approach path, where they could bring down an airliner. Hundreds of milling geese stay grounded in the meadow today, while off in the northeastern corner, three coyotes prowl for game. One bounds high as if performing the ballet fantastique, then pounces on something. A mole, I hope.

The Peninsula Canal dead-ends at the Columbia Edgewater Country Club, close to NE Marine Drive. I veer onto the golf course, crossing beautifully landscaped grounds and heading toward the far perimeter, which adjoins the Flyway Wetlands. The Edgewater's heavily forested course holds over two hundred legacy giant sequoias. The club's official motto is "Keep calm and go long."

When the course is too crowded, I veer further south onto the maintenance road. The road stops at a tall cyclone fence with a locked gate that blocks access into a residential neighborhood. Getting over the fence isn't easy.

Laura O. Foster—author of several Portland walking guides— once accompanied me on this route. The fence was no problem for her. Fit and agile, she scaled it with the ease of a mountain panther. Not I. My boots were muddy, so I couldn't get a good purchase. Laura stood on the other side, laughing.

"Try harder," she said.

I tried harder, embarrassed myself, and gave up, lurching like a drunken Sasquatch through dense foliage next to a private residence. Breaking free from a holly bush, I tromped across a daffodil bed into the street.

"A woman in the house was watching you from the upstairs window," said Laura. "And she wasn't smiling."

Today, golfers are sparse, so I avoid the fence and cut straight across the Edgewater. Entering the East Columbia neighborhood (listed as Portland's eighty-sixth most walkable), I cross a grassy dike on the twenty-three–acre Flyway Wetlands. A network of south-facing gravel bars forms bioengineered turtle habitats. Next to a shallow pond, a belted kingfisher chitters from a stand of cattails. Ducks take flight. Likely gadwalls and northern shovelers.

Reaching solid ground on NE 13th Ave, I head for the Columbia Children's Arboretum, one of Portland's least-known pocket parks. Tucked back into the surrounding neighborhood, it's not easy to find. Somebody keeps removing the park signs.

Turning down the street leading to the Children's Arboretum, I see a gigantic American flag fluttering in a front yard, dwarfing the house. A lawn sign posted near the flagpole reads: "ANYONE FOUND HERE AT NIGHT WILL BE FOUND HERE IN THE MORNING." A photo of an AR-15 appears below the message.

The Columbia Children's Arboretum is a green oasis in an industrialized desert. A great spot for a pastoral stroll. A shady pathway skirts a side channel of the slough, a place where stout ranks of oaks, maples, cedars, and pines show off their spring green. In the 1970s, Portland Public School children wrote letters to all fifty governors of the land, requesting their state trees for the park. A tall order to squeeze a United States of Trees into twenty-seven acres, but many local volunteers made it happen. As I walk, I admire North Carolina's longleaf pine, New Hampshire's paper birch, Oklahoma's eastern redbud, and Tennessee's tulip poplar. Like all good trees, they purify water, clean the air, beautify the landscape, and shelter wildlife. The Children's Arboretum has a dash of magic in it. Walking through this treescape feels like passing a portal into a new and improved world.

Not ready to leave, I rest on a picnic bench and consider the best route home. I hate backtracking but making a loop requires a long trek through grim industrial neighborhoods. Reluctantly, I decide to deadhead home.

An hour later, I'm back on NE 33rd Drive, where a pile of roadside garbage greets me. Food wrappers and a dirty diaper spill out from a black trash sack. On a mattress, a moldy teddy bear sprawls face down, as if recovering from a night of binge drinking. Even before tent and RV camps landed here, this transportation corridor doubled as a public dump. In pre-COVID times, inmate crews in orange suits collected roadside trash. Often more trash reappeared overnight.

Americans shed possessions faster than a snake sheds its skin. I try to imagine what hides deep beneath the roadside squalor. From his grave, Walt Whitman would urge me to grab a shovel and dig past the surface of things. "If you want me again," he wrote in *Leaves of Grass*, "look for me under your boot soles." Digging here, perhaps I'd find a wagon spoke, a brass spittoon, a carburetor, a DDT canister. Maybe a vaping pipe. But no dead poets.

Almost home, I lean on the bridge spanning the Columbia Slough and gaze at the shady expanse of slack water. By anyone's reckoning, the slough teems with environmental bugbears and bugaboos.

Even so, the wild animals of the slough go about their business, adapting to the constant encroachments of human activities. Right now, I see three male wigeons floating out from beneath the bridge, their green and cream-colored heads bobbing as they dabble for pondweed. These ducks, which a friend calls "baldpates," don't look worried about anything except maybe staying a safe distance from predators.

Recently, I learned a Latin phrase: *ignis fatuus*. A slippery mouthful of vowels and consonants. The Merriam-Webster dictionary says it means "foolish fire" and refers to "light that sometimes appears in marshy ground . . . attributable to the combustion of gas from organic matter." The phrase also describes "a deceptive goal or hope."

For me, ignis fatuus describes our current environmental emergency. We're all fools on fire, hoping to gain "dominion over the fish of the sea and over the birds of the sky . . . and every creeping thing that creeps on earth."

Back at home, I check my phone for distance walked. Eight miles. Not enough to blow off anger over the dead flicker. Maybe a backbreaking session of yard yoga will mellow me out—a few hard hours of pulling weeds, leaving me too tired to rage about feral cats, dead birds, or climate change.

13 NEIGHBORS

> You don't have to love your neighbor. Just leave him alone.

MARTY RUBIN, *BOILED FROG SYNDROME*

. . .

JUST AFTER DUSK on a January weekend, four men in hazmat suits hoisted klieg lights over our driveway. A fire truck idled behind two utility trucks. A couple of beefy firefighters leaned against their truck and unwrapped sandwiches from aluminum foil. *Why is the fire engine still running?* I wondered. The hazmat guys flipped a switch, and harsh white light flooded our home. It looked like a crime scene, complete with yellow caution tape strung around the trench at our driveway.

"Let's go in," I said, leaning on Bruce's shoulder. "I can't stand to look at this anymore."

Hours earlier, the three trucks had barreled down our street to confront the disaster scene at our place. Hopping out, the utility guys zipped into white jumpsuits, pulling hoods with clear visors over their heads. Then they'd disappeared into the trench.

The rest of the afternoon, Bruce and I paced inside, awaiting the verdict. Not a single neighbor had emerged from their home to walk the short distance to the dead end, knock on our door, ask questions, or inspect the scene. Not even at dusk, with their own water cut off for hours, and klieg lights illuminating the street. After a year of living among these neighbors, I no longer wondered why.

The summer before, our first garden exploded with produce. Giant cabbages and spinach, mesclun, snow peas, broccoli, green onions, carrots, tomatoes, and peppers—everything but eggplant and turnips thrived. I harvested, hand washed, and bagged colorful mixes of greens, onions, and peas to bring to our neighbors. But all down the street, no one answered my knocks, despite multiple cars parked in driveways. The next morning, I gave the vegetables to my coworkers.

At Christmas, we'd tried again. Our daughter Miranda baked chocolate chip cookies, which she arranged on red paper plates covered with cling wrap labeled "Merry Xmas from the Henry/Campbells." After a second unanswered knock, she left cookies on several front stoops. Only our closest neighbor returned the greetings with fudge brownies.

Now it was late January. I closed the shades on the hazmat men and opened a bottle of wine.

"Are you hungry?" I asked Bruce.

"Nope. Your burger's still stuck in my belly."

With our water cut off, hamburger grease had congealed around pickle juice on the piled-up lunch dishes. I poured Bruce a full glass of red wine, and we sat on the couch to puzzle over where we'd gone wrong. At eleven p.m., I took one more peek through the blinds before we collapsed into bed, a little drunk. Klieg lights still flooded the street. The men in hazmat suits remained in the trench, their welding arc throwing off white hot sparks.

The dry winter morning had begun well, with our friend Scott visiting from New England. A few months earlier, the city had paved our dirt stub road, and we got a notice requiring us to decommission our septic tank. We'd have to hook up to Portland's sewer lines. Now Bruce and Scott, two sixty-something college friends, prepared to roll up their sleeves and dig a six-foot-deep trench for a sewer line from the driveway into our south yard. Scott's son-in-law Andrew, a local plumber's apprentice, would lay the pipes.

By mid-morning, Scott, Bruce, and Andrew were already leaning on their shovels, panting from hacking out the hard-packed clay.

"Why don't we rent a Bobcat from up on Columbia?" Bruce suggested. "Hand digging is going to take days."

"No use breaking your backs," I called out from the side door. "Get the Bobcat and I'll start making lunch." The three of them tossed their shovels out of the ditch.

An hour later, with Andrew at the throttle, the Bobcat was making speedy work excavating the trench. I was broiling burgers and slicing pickles and onions, timing lunch to when they'd finish. Then I heard a loud "Mother-fxxk!" Cracking the door open, I saw water gushing into the trench—the Bobcat's shovel had sliced our water main.

"I'm gonna shut the water off!" Andrew yelled, jumping off the Bobcat. "I can fix this. No problem."

As he located the shut-off valve, I ran out with a camera to capture a shot of Scott scowling in the trench, water rising up his calves. He frowned at me like, "You're documenting THIS?" It seemed like the right time to call the men in to lunch.

I take some blame for what happened next. Beside the burgers, I set cold beers in front of the guys. As they ate, Andrew cast anxious glances at Scott, who remained the picture of tight-lipped New England stoicism. Scott was a calm man with deep expertise building commercial structures and restoring historic homes. Over lunch, he and Bruce rehashed stories of camping together, flat-broke, in their twenties. Their laughter cut the tension at the table.

"At least I didn't hit the gas line," said Andrew suddenly, apropos of nothing. "That would've been real trouble."

I served him a second burger. Thinking to settle his nerves, I set another beer alongside Andrew's plate. Bruce frowned at me.

Ten minutes after the plates were cleared and Andrew had remounted the Bobcat, two man-screams jolted me up and out.

"He's hit the gas line!" yelled Bruce. Through the open side door, I heard the unmistakable hiss of gas bubbling through water in the trench, less than ten feet away.

"Where's the nearest hardware store?" yelled Scott. "We need a clamp to tie off the gas!"

"Back in fifteen minutes," he said after getting directions to Lowe's. "We can fix this. No need to call the gas company!"

As Scott and Andrew peeled out, the air outside our back door filled with the rotten-egg smell of mercaptan, the sulfurous chemical added to natural gas, which is odorless, as an alert to leaks. Gas bubbles popped at the trench water's surface.

"Aren't gas and water a dangerous combo?" I asked Bruce. "We could be endangering the neighbors."

I went inside to pace. Behind one knotty pine cabinet I found a sticker: "Smell gas? Call 1-800-XXXX immediately."

"How do we even know they can get the right part?" I asked twenty minutes later, in a strangulated voice. In their haste, Scott and Andrew had left their phones behind.

"If this thing explodes," said Bruce, dead calm, "it will take our house down."

My heart pounded as I opened the screen door to check for human activity. Except for the hissing time bomb, the street was quiet. Nobody seemed to notice that our neighborhood teetered on the edge of disaster.

At twenty-five minutes, I announced, "I'm calling the gas company. It's the law."

Five minutes later, two natural gas trucks careened in, yellow lights flashing. Scott and Andrew were close behind. They leaped out of Andrew's car with a bag of clamps in hand just as a fire truck closed in behind their car.

Kicking gravel, Andrew spoke briefly to the hazmat men. Then he came inside with Scott and collapsed on our couch, hobbled by hamstring cramps.

"I'm not cut out to be a plumber," he moaned. "I'm done for."

"Get a hold of yourself," Scott hissed through lower teeth, chewing his handlebar mustache. "You're an adult. Act like it."

Andrew wiped his face and asked if we had any marijuana. "I need something to relax. I'm about to climb out of my skin." Weed was not yet legal in Oregon, but I remembered a friend's half-smoked joint from a summer party tucked in the back of a drawer. I dug it out and handed it over. Shortly after, the two of them took off for Andrew's house. There was nothing more they could do.

The next morning, a Sunday, our house was still standing, and water and gas were back on in the neighborhood. Scott and Andrew showed up late morning looking haggard and hungover. Together, we figured out what went wrong. We'd correctly contacted the Dig Right contractors to locate and mark gas and water lines prior to digging. Andrew had used their spray-painted marks to guide his dig. What none of us had noticed was that Dig Right had not finished the job. We found a small handwritten note tacked to a wood stake, promising to return on Monday to finish marking the lines.

It was an expensive miss. A few weeks later, the City of Portland sent us a $3,000 fine for gas line repairs—including labor and overtime pay for the four employees, who had finally emerged from the trench after midnight.

We didn't see Scott or Andrew for a few years after that, and this incident has yet to become one we've laughed about together.

But all is well with our friendship, and Andrew's now a sought-after licensed plumber. He and Scott still work together.

But this is more a story about our neighbors. Not one of them ever asked questions or mentioned the gas-line fiasco to us. None of them had walked down the street that long day to investigate. In our former neighborhood, we couldn't plant a pansy without someone wandering over for a "Whatcha up to?" chat.

The folks who live in the fourteen homes on our street are a diverse lot of homeowners and renters—young musicians, tech and health care workers, blue-collar laborers, small business owners, and retirees. A few store boats and RVs on large lots; many hunt and fish. Our houses range from ramshackle to solidly middle class. One is a double-wide modular home on a full acre lot. Another is a tiny, dilapidated rental with a roof that's gone to moss. People are cordial, but mostly they keep to themselves.

Rarely do police cars patrol our quiet street. Recorded crime stats in the Sunderland neighborhood are much lower than the more populous neighborhoods to the south—over a recent two-year period, one or two carjackings and a domestic violence report.

Still, at times offenses do occur. A few years ago, someone shot a coyote, leaving its bloody carcass on the tenth green, next to our house. Another neighbor burns his trash at night. Two others make money rehabbing vehicles to sell. Half-stripped car skeletons dot the hill up to Columbia Blvd.

On summer evenings, random rifle shots ring out from the dilapidated rentals up the hill. The wind carries their loud family squabbles down to us. The "Pallet People" we've named this group, for the teetering stacks of wooden platforms they sell off the back of an old truck.

One day, I stopped my car to say hello to Pallet Woman. She walked toward me wearing a pink-stringed halter top that hung loose off a bony body that might've topped ninety pounds. From a distance, she looked like a teenager with long blondish hair, flip-flops, and cut-off shorts hugging cute legs. But close in, I noticed the missing teeth, lines etched around her mouth and dark eye circles. She could've been forty. She could've been sixty. But she was pleasant and chattered nonstop about outsmarting her landlord who wanted to tear their house down and sell the property for industrial development.

The city's proposal to rezone our neighborhood and parts of the golf course to "industrial sanctuary" sparked little passion on our block. I placed flyers summarizing the issues in each mailbox and invited neighbors down to our place for snacks and beverages to discuss strategy. Only one showed up. The next morning, I took the chips, dips, and cheese into work. Bruce and I drank the wine.

Life on the slough is an ongoing clash of industry with open space. On our block, there are trade-offs for our large lots and bountiful wildlife. Getting off our street safely onto NE 33rd is one of these.

Up the hill from us, the dangerous interchange at Columbia Blvd. has caused several accidents, some with injuries and at least two fatalities. Large trucks get stuck trying to make the sharp curve over NE 33rd's seismically unsafe ramp. Walkers and bicyclists have no crosswalks, lights, or other safe way across Columbia and Lombard Blvds. These roads, with railroad tracks separating them, create more than a physical barrier between the denser neighborhoods to the south and our homes scattered across the Columbia River floodplain. They pose a psychic barrier too. We're the folks who live on the wrong side of the tracks.

With just over seven hundred residents the Sunderland neighborhood is low density, its isolated pockets of homes and apartments hugging the river and parts of the slough. More people work here than live here. Twice as many people of color per capita live along Columbia/Lombard corridors as in the rest of the city. Child poverty rates are high. In 2020, median house prices in Sunderland were below $250K. We have no active neighborhood association.

A mile away and uncounted in the Sunderland census live scores of people in dilapidated RVs and vehicles strung out along NE 33rd Drive. Riding my bike to Marine Drive, I counted sixty vehicles over a half-mile stretch. They range from burned and stripped-out hulks to full-size RVs with generators attached. Makeshift tents and tarps extend onto the Port of Portland's meadows. Trash spills out and piles up. On dry days, denizens move outside, rearrange possessions and tinker under hoods. As any Portlander knows, the growing number of unhoused folks is not unique to our neighborhood.

Just across the meadow west of these vehicles, Dignity Village's colorful tiny houses offer one solution to the housing crisis. Operating since 2000 on city-owned land, the Village's well-maintained homes house about sixty adults for up to two years each. The first "village"-model shelter in North America, Dignity Village is self-governed and self-operated. A few of the homes are connected to electricity. Showers, sinks, and portable toilets are shared. Community rules keep the peace.

Next to Dignity Village, two inmates at the Columbia River Correctional Institution climbed a fence a few years ago and walked through the woods to the levee above Peninsula Canal. One was caught hours later at the Jack-in-a-Box on MLK Blvd. After that, NO TRESPASSING signs were posted below the levee.

In the years since the gas-line fiasco, our neighbors have grown more sociable. Two millennial couples bought homes down the block. We invited one couple for lunch, serving them a botched potato soup, which they finished politely. In April, our next-door neighbors brought fresh trout caught off their new boat, and we reciprocated with asparagus, cucumbers, and salad greens. But mostly, we relished being left to ourselves to roam and work our property. Early mornings during the worst of COVID, I toured the garden in my ratty red robe, thinking that maybe next summer I'd set a table at the end of the street. I'd put a wicker basket on top and tape on a sign that says:

"HEY, NEIGHBORS: Help yourself to homegrown veggies. Stay healthy. Stay safe!"

14 THE MOLE CHI MINH TRAIL

All but blind
in his chambered hole,
Gropes for worms
the four-clawed mole.

WALTER DE LA MARE, "ALL BUT
BLIND," *COLLECTED POEMS*
1901-1918

. . .

MOLES. Ugh. You always know when they come calling. The ground erupts like a bad case of teenage acne. Moles are the death of landscaping. Stomp on one mole mound and three more pop up elsewhere. At night, press an ear to bare earth and you can eavesdrop on them. Their digging gives off a low graveyard grumble. Creepy. Imagine a corpse mumbling inside a casket.

Mole tunnels boobytrap our garden and lawn. Walking on seemingly solid ground, I sometimes plunge calf-deep into a multi-layered network of tunnels, opening a huge cavern into the vast underground mole empire. Six feet beneath my boot, the hefty Townsend's mole *(Scapanus townsendii)* rules every cubic centimeter it travels. Though it averages only six inches in length, a mole can lift dirt twenty times its weight to create a vast network of tunnels that undercuts the foundations of plants, shrubs, and trees.

Deploying its stubby spade-shaped paws, the Townsend's mole burrows over a hundred feet a day, creating dark, dry air pockets where plant roots dangle and die of thirst. Over one day, zinnias and dahlias will wither. Even worse, voles (a cousin of the field mouse) commandeer mole tunnels to devour tubers, bulbs, and roots.

One day, I tried to flush out a particularly bothersome mole with a high-pressure blast of water from my garden hose. It worked. The mole erupted from the muddy froth like a Polaris missile, gnashing spike-like incisors at me. To protect myself, I kept blasting it. The mole just twisted around in mid-air and dove back in, breaking the surface without even a telltale gurgle.

Like badgers and meerkats, moles follow a "fossorial lifestyle," which is science-speak for any creature that likes to dig deep into the earth. The only eco-benefit I can see they deliver is that as moles devour slugs and Japanese beetle grubs, they plow up the soil, aerating and fertilizing it. True enough, but while it's doing that, one measly mole can also deep six a garden's earthly treasures. Where's the benefit in that?

In Kenneth Grahame's children's book *The Wind in the Willows*, Mole is a beloved character. Grahame describes Mole as a dreamer who "bitterly accepts the hard, cold waking and all its penalties." Such sentimentality has no truck with me. Real moles—not imaginary ones—wreck my garden.

Moles stuff their guts with muddy grubs and worms. They wouldn't make a casting call for a Disney cartoon. With squinty eyes, no dimples, and a scary-looking snout, they're not very telegenic. What endearing characteristics do moles convey? Most likely blind devotion to duty. They dutifully destroy yards. Especially ours.

Each day, I fight a whack-a-mole war. In their quest for food, the little dirt tossers usually strike at night, leaving Vesuvian mounds of dirt that upend our collards and kale. Like unwanted house guests, they never leave, feasting on an all-you-can-eat smorgasbord of earthworms, grubs, and beetles. Serpentine ridges of soil mark off their subterranean route, a clod-shaped calligraphy denoting gluttony. Moles belong to the scientific order *Eulipotyphla,* which in Latin means "truly fat and blind." Appropriate.

One day we were walking our property when our new dog, Gracie, rammed her snout into a mound of dirt and came up with a mole. I saw only the blur of a little gray tail before she swallowed the mole whole. She probably didn't even taste it. Lucky for her. William Buckland, a Victorian Age theologian-geologist, bragged about eating his way through the animal kingdom. He reportedly claimed the blue bottlefly and the mole had the most displeasing tastes of any creature that landed on his dinner plate.

In my observation, predators don't dine on moles much. Coyotes, hawks, and herons snag them occasionally, but these slippery dirt munchers zip from sight as fast as gaper clams on the Oregon coast. Predators probably consider fish, frogs, and rabbits easier to catch—and more pleasing to the palate.

One afternoon Miranda spotted a mole wandering along a wire mesh fence that bordered our property. Why was it out in broad daylight? Was it sick? Suddenly, a sharp-shinned hawk swooped in and landed on the other side of the fence. Extending one set of talons through the wire mesh, it seized the mole. The little hawk tried pulling its prey through the fence, but the mole was too fat to fit. The hawk kept trying. No go. Finally, it screeched, released its catch, and flew off in search of more catchable prey. The mole, delivered from death row, dug double time into the dirt and vanished.

I complained about my mole problem to a gardener friend. "Piss down their holes," she advised. "Works for me."

This folk remedy relies on the firepower of a full bladder—many full bladders. I considered inviting friends over for an all-night beer fest but rejected this idea. Drunken mole dousers with piss-poor aim might send my soil pH off the scale.

Biologists call the mole an insectivore. In its oxygen-deficient lair, it tolerates high levels of carbon dioxide. It has weak eyes, but an olfactory adaptation called stereo sniffing enables it to quickly geolocate the goodies. A toxin in mole saliva paralyzes its prey. Moles stash away stupefied earthworms and return later to eat them. Before tucking into a meal, the mole patiently squeezes the grit from the earthworm's guts, then chews everything into bite-sized bits. Reminds me of the 1956 low-budget movie *Mole People*. One of its publicity posters reads: "From a Lost Age . . . Horror Crawls from the Depths of the Earth!"

Unless it's mating season, moles are loners. They avoid their own kind and drive off interlopers. Moles are polygynandrous, meaning that females mate with multiple males in an apparent attempt to deepen the gene pool. The offspring are born bald and pink. After maturing, the youngsters must find their own turf. They hardly ever fail in this. Our half-acre property is a sizable chunk of real estate for a crew of grouchy, antisocial moles to bulldoze like the Army Corps of Berserkers.

Practitioners of English folk medicine considered moles useful in treating many physical ailments. To cure rheumatism, people carried amputated mole paws in their pockets. To combat goiter, they skinned moles and tied the bodies around their necks.

Pliny the Elder's *Naturalis Historia* (AD 77) mentions that magicians recommended swallowing a palpitating mole heart to produce "the power of divination and foreknowledge of future events." Did a mole heart predict the fall of the Roman Empire?

Moles may represent a miracle cure for maladies, but for me, they're underground guerrillas. Never taking a breather, they tunnel through our terrain, leaving what I call the "Mole Chi Minh Trail."

During the Vietnam War, the ten-thousand-mile Ho Chi Minh Trail provided the People's Army of the North passage into South Vietnam. The American military carpet-bombed the trail and defoliated the jungle, using six hundred thousand gallons of "rainbow herbicides," including Agent Orange. Nothing worked. Exhibiting tenacity and logistical legerdemain, the North's leader, Ho Chi Minh, outsmarted the Pentagon's whiz kids, and the People's Army prevailed.

One day, we discovered how the vast multi-level network of mole tunnels was more extensive than we'd ever imagined. Somehow, our neighbor's kitten, who was usually out stalking sparrows or pouncing on butterflies and newborn voles, had squirmed into a tunnel in our yard and couldn't find its way out. Nancy and I kept hearing its piteous cries beneath the ground. "M-E-O-O-O-W! M-E-O-O-O-W!" For three nights and days it kept up a spooky subterranean moan.

On the fourth morning, I put my ear to the ground, listening to the trapped kitten's cries. They were getting weaker. I picked up a shovel and started digging up our yard, uprooting ferns, flowers, shrubs, and small trees. I'd injured my back recently, so Nancy and our neighbor joined in. Soon, our yard was a disaster scene of dirt, rocks, and tree roots, but we still couldn't find the kitten. Maybe we'd driven it deeper into the maze of mole tunnels.

Exhausted after two hours of digging, we gave up. Nancy and I went into the house for a drink of water, and our neighbor and her kids returned home, her daughter in tears. A short time later, we heard the teenager shouting that the kitten had somehow freed itself and was now clinging to a high cedar branch that overhung the hummocks of upturned earth. The cedar was too gnarly to scale, and nobody had a ladder long enough to reach the kitty. Finally, like a volunteer firefighter, I used my pole pruner, telescoped out to its full length, to saw the limb that held our quarry. When the branch snapped free, the kitten toppled from the supporting boughs and fell safely into a fishing net my neighbor's son held. A happy ending for all. I picked up a shovel and began putting our yard back together.

One kitten saved, yet our mole enemy persisted. Since my adversary tipped the scales at just about four ounces, cluster bombs and napalm weren't appropriate. Nor would I use chemicals that would poison soil and water.

In the beginning, my weapons of choice included commercial repellents, ultrasonic spikes, and scissor traps. Hardware stores hawk tons of this sort of stuff. It's all a waste of money. The kill-a-mole market has spawned many millionaires, and multitudes of moles still thrive. In exasperation, I stomp on mole mounds, caving in their tunnels, but the little buggers always dig an alternate route. Lately, I concoct my own mole-be-gone products. Usually a blend of coffee grounds, castor oil, vinegar, blood meal, and red pepper flakes, but the moles remain the undisputed masters of the underworld.

Repel a mole, and it returns with reinforcements. Kill one, and a replacement shows up yesterday. Improving soil fertility—thereby increasing the number of worms—sends moles into full feeding frenzy mode. The ground beneath my feet is the crumbling roof of a gigantic mole condo. Vacancies are rare. The mole reigns sub-ternal.

As a rearguard action in the garden, I built raised beds with untreated wood frames and metal mesh bottoms. In a damp climate, even cedar rots, enabling moles to squirm between small gaps in metal and wood. Eventually I was able to make several mole-proof garden beds from large, galvanized tubs. Problem is, while the tubs thwart the moles they also isolate the soil, cutting off free movement of microorganisms and macroinvertebrates. Plants prefer to sink their roots into unrestricted ground where they can socialize more freely with their neighbors—and develop effective defenses against invasive organisms.

At night, I stress about the dark army of earth movers toiling beneath the topsoil. Will these creatures ever stop digging and eating? Don't they ever get tired—or bored? How do they manage to mate blindly in the dark? Do they grapple with weighty philosophical thoughts? Like *I dig, therefore I am?*

Marc Hamer, author of *How to Catch a Mole: Wisdom from a Life Lived in Nature*, sums it all up. "Moles are tiny, they are cute, and like the rest of nature they do not care what we feel. They are devastating, and they always win."

15 STUCK IN THE MUD

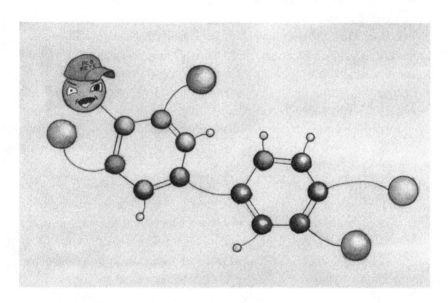

66 **Poisoning water is an assassination.**

JACQUES-YVES COUSTEAU, "STATEMENT
TO THE TWELFTH MEETING WITH THE
PANEL OF SCIENCE AND TECHNOLOGY"

. . .

THE FIRST NIGHTMARE woke me soon after Bruce got stuck in the slough. He'd borrowed our neighbor Dan's hip waders to have another go at the late summer algae, a perpetual problem before the culvert replacement. From the safety of the dock, I watched Bruce slog out six feet to angle the lake rake over the mat, gnats swirling around the fetid carpet. Suddenly, he halted, and I knew something was wrong.

"I'm stuck!" he yelled. "I can barely lift my feet."

I leaned out over the dock and grabbed the rake handle from him. "Give it up! Come back in." I watched in fascinated horror as he struggled to move.

"I lost Dan's boot cover!" He sounded dazed. "The mud sucked it right off." By the time he slowly slogged back to shore, he was sweating. "I'm not trying that again," he panted.

Later that fall, when the rains had still not arrived and the mudflat expanded out from the dock, Bruce drove a six-foot prybar over and over into the dense muck, hoping to snag out the boot cover. No sign of it anywhere. Like quicksand in a horror movie, the sediments had swallowed it forever.

In my nightmare that night, I'm paddling east toward the end of Buffalo Slough, when my kayak snags on a fallen willow branch, flips, and I spill out into murky waist-deep water, churning up clouds of silt as my feet sink deeply into mud. The sediments cling like iron filings to a magnet and harden into concrete around my calves. I cannot lift my anchored legs, and I'm too far from shore to be heard by anyone. My body grows rigid from fright. Finally, toe cramps in both feet awaken me.

My fears about the sediments were fact-based. A little knowledge proved a frightening thing. After settling into our new home, I began to study the slough's long history as an open sewer, toxic waste dump, and repository of chemical-laden stormwater. I learned that sediments, even more than water, trap and hold onto the poisons of industry and farming. The worst of these were the notoriously tenacious PCBs (polychlorinated biphenyls), compounds of highly toxic organic chlorine. PCBs were created in the 1920s and widely used as machinery lubricants and coolants until they were banned in 1979.

Gazing north from our bedroom window a few weeks after the nightmare, I saw that the water was deep, the mud safely out of sight. The surface looked like a polished mirror. The buffleheads, my favorite diving ducks, had arrived for the winter. Comically round like rubber duckies, they bob high in the water, feathery spheres of buoyant black and white. They do a cute disappearing act as they dive for insects and pondweeds and then bounce up again several seconds later, yards away. Through the winter, other migrant divers join them—smoky ring-necked ducks with milky bills, elegant, red-breasted mergansers and golden-eyes, white circles flanking their beaks. Mergansers glide through the water like sleek ocean liners. When they dive, they barely cleave the water.

I am always entertained by the pageant outside our windows— the succession of migratory birds drawn to the wetlands. Lots of crayfish and freshwater mussels for otters, raccoons, and stoats. Life thrives here, despite the slough's toxic buffet of chemicals. Abundant grasses—wild, invasive, and manicured—line the canals, woods, and golf course. They feed the ubiquitous Canada geese but also scores of other herbivores such as rabbits, deer, muskrats, and nutria. Late at night, coyotes yip and howl in a joyous chorus, hunting the fields where rabbits, voles and moles abound.

This "industrial sanctuary" has many downsides, yet where else in the city could we live among so much nature?

But all the years we'd lived slough-side, I'd avoided any direct contact with the mud that spreads from our dock. I realized finally I needed to face my fear of the sediments. Get to know them better from the safe distance of research.

I began with the word "sediment." It comes from the Latin *sedere*, which means to sit or settle. A synonym is "dregs." I like the word *dregs*—it suggests the last pour from a bottle of red wine. Or a smoky medieval tavern, where yeasty meads leave suspicious solids in mugs drained by yeomen with beet-colored faces.

Sediments are made from rocks, clay, sand, and minerals mixed with the remains of plants and animals. While soil formation requires a stable surface to build upon, sediments are nomadic. They move around, are picked up and dropped into place by ice, rivers, rain, and wind. Erosion carries them along, and chemical reactions with water distills them out.

Sediments can be as large as a boulder, or as small as a grain of sand. In the Buffalo Slough, they have their own character—fine and silty, and several feet deep. When Bruce drove his prybar into the mud off the dock, it sank nearly to his knuckles. The year before, we'd hired our friend Dude to replace the Gieses' decrepit dock. Setting in new concrete pilings, he'd called up to where I was watching from the deck. "This is WEIRD! The mud is sticking fast to the post. It's helping me do the job."

When exposed by low water, the slough banks look like creamy peanut butter, dotted with golf balls and cross-hatched with geese, duck, and raccoon tracks. The nutrias carve muddy slides from the water through the blackberry thickets up to the golf course where they nibble the grass down to the roots. At the shoreline, water striders skitter across the mud, and freshwater mussels exposed to air burrow deeper to dodge the raccoons, which pluck them out to crack and eat, scattering empty shells across The Bog.

I wanted to know how slough sediments had changed since clean-up efforts had intensified over the past decade. So, I went online to get 2018's Columbia Slough Sediment Data Analysis Report, hot off the press from Oregon DEQ (Department of Environmental Quality). The report promised a comprehensive study of sediments dredged from each of the slough's reaches.

Earlier studies in 1994 and 2006 showed widespread contamination throughout the slough. In 1994, Buffalo Slough sediments were especially high in heavy metals (lead, copper, and zinc). Anglers were warned of significant risk from PCBs and pesticides (e.g., DDT, chlordane, dieldrin). Alarmingly, 2006 data reported even higher levels of contamination.

To get the latest report online required me to "Explain how your document request will serve the public good" and then asked what I planned to do with the information. Annoyed, I tapped out a terse, "I'm a resident and stakeholder of the slough." I stopped myself from adding, "'Nuff said."

When the report was finally emailed, the download took several minutes. It was two thousand pages with appendices and lists of acronyms and abbreviations. Armed with a rainbow of digital highlighters, I spent a full week going through it.

The study analyzed 102 sediment samples taken from eight reaches along the lower, middle, and upper sloughs, mostly using a large Ekman dredge, which captures matter to a depth of ten centimeters. Happily, Buffalo Slough was included in the sampling.

Slough reports tell a true crime story. It's a complex tale whose plot unfolds at a glacial pace, revealing evidence collected and trends analyzed over time. The crime scene is rife with incriminating—often startling—forensic data. And sediments are a prosecutor's dream. Mud cannot lie, and it clings fast to critical details. Unfortunately, sediments rarely reveal their sources.

The major crimes against the slough occurred in dozens of locations throughout the twentieth century. Given the scope, complexity, and long period of time, it's a wonder that investigators didn't call it quits, leaving behind a cold case. But in fact, as of this writing, ongoing environmental investigations analyze both water and sediments throughout the slough. Numerous parties collaborate to improve conditions, including government, property owners, scientists, environmental groups, and water/soil consultants. DEQ provides overall direction, commissions studies and partners with Portland's Bureau of Environmental Services (BES) to oversee and monitor the remedies. All these partners play critical roles.

That said, nothing is crystal clear about the slough (pun intended). Today, historic perpetrators of pollution sponsor slough conservation fundraisers and sign contracts with the government to clean up their messes. At annual watershed council dinners, they click glasses and applaud slide and video presentations that celebrate recovery successes.

For a layperson trying to make sense of the sediment story, the scientific terms threatened to overwhelm the narrative. So I cheat-sheeted key acronyms and abbreviations:

- COPC: Contaminants of Potential Concern
- CFOE: Cumulative Factors of Exceedance
- SLV: Screening Level Values

I learned that when COPCs and CFOEs show up together, that spells trouble, signaling sediments layered with too much and too many of the manufactured substances that fertilize farms and golf courses, lubricate engine parts, deice jets, fabricate metals, and more. The toxic hazards vary widely but all of them pose clear harm to living things.

Sediment nasties appear in three main flavors: heavy metals (lead, copper, zinc, mercury); pesticides (DDT, DDE, and chlordane); and PCBs. All three types of contaminants are bound in a devil's triangle of deposition.

For most of the twentieth century, the slough was used to move logs, dump sewage, water crops, and absorb runoff from Portland's burgeoning industry and commerce. Standard practice for a new American community trying to tame the wilderness and beat a living from the land. Slaughterhouses, meatpacking plants, tanneries, and sawmills clustered near the Willamette River along the lower slough. One of these businesses, the Swift Meats plant in Kenton, employed more than 1,500 workers and butchered more beef than any other town in the Northwest. To the east, along the narrower middle and upper sloughs, bucolic farms, orchards, and ranches prevailed.

Decades later, the sediment residues of agriculture and industry stratify geographically. DDT, DDE and chlordane show up in the upper and middle sloughs, where chemically maintained lawns and golf courses overtook the farms and orchards that first introduced these toxins. In the lower slough, where auto wrecking, metal and pipe shops still operate, the PCB lubricants used by these businesses appear in greater concentrations.

Commercial boat traffic ended on the slough more than a half century ago. Shortly after, the city stopped dredging the Peninsula Canal, and it silted shut for good. Now, the city only dredges sediments at highly contaminated hotspots. Otherwise, most of the slough's forty-plus miles of channel bottoms remain undisturbed under low gradient, slow-moving waters. Over the decades these sediments have settled out, settled in, and made cozy with an ongoing stream of pollutants and pathogens.

In the middle and upper sloughs, only the wind, stormwater

outfalls, a handful of springs, and the drainage pumps move water. Tidal action from the Willamette River lifts the lower slough up and down, and kayakers are advised to check tide tables to avoid stranding near the shallow Smith and Bybee Lakes. Up or down, no direct connection remains of slough waters with the Columbia River.

In the early nineties, the state of the slough sullied Portland's growing reputation as an ecotopia. In 1993, the Portland City Council voted to spend $125 million to eliminate all combined sewer overflows to the slough. This was a critical first step in an uphill battle, as the slough watershed still hosted most of Portland's heavy industry.

The St. Johns Landfill, a garbage dump built directly on top of Smith and Bybee Lakes, finally closed in 1991. It was too full to hold more garbage. Though sewage no longer discharged directly into the slough, some businesses continued to dump factory wastes into its waters throughout the nineties.

In 1994, DEQ gave the slough a failing grade for water quality, noting problems like low oxygen and high toxicity, bacteria, phosphorus, pH, and temperature levels. That same year, the Oregon Health Division issued its first warning about consuming slough fish, based on elevated PCBs and pesticides in catches near the St. Johns Landfill. The first $100 million allocated to slough cleanup went quickly, but at last, the tide was turning.

Unfortunately, total cleanup of slough sediments isn't possible. Dredging is expensive and creates its own problems—chiefly finding a place to bury contaminated sludge. The slough watershed drains nearly 33,000 acres of land, much of it owned by chemical-dependent industries. Even if all its contaminated sediments could be capped or safely removed, new toxins would still arrive from stormwater runoff, upland soils, and dozens of outfalls. Pinning down responsible parties poses a continuing challenge when runoff from multiple businesses may enter the slough through a single outfall.

With limited resources, DEQ prioritizes three goals: controlling pollution from upland sources; cleaning up and remediating hot spots; and monitoring water, sediments, and fish over the long term.

In 2008, a new settlement process required slough polluters to pay into a remediation fund. Their payments were based on estimated costs to investigate and clean up their properties. A bit of a win for polluters who could then avoid the expense of conducting their own investigations. Near us, the McBride and Whitaker Ponds settlements show how this process works from investigation to cleanup. More on Whitaker follows.

In our own small ways, we've tried to help. Early on, Bruce planted willows around the dock, training branches over the water to provide cooling shade for fish and other aquatic life. From the woods, he clipped red osier dogwood stakes and drove them into slough banks where they found water and rooted. Red osier dogwood sequesters heavy metals (but not PCBs).

Working with the Columbia Slough Watershed Council, Bruce and other volunteers uprooted loads of invasive ivy and blackberries off the Buffalo Slough slopes. And a small grant to the Council funded more volunteers to plant native shrubs like snowberry, twinberry, and Oregon grape along the Buffalo's north bank.

I was heartened by 2018's report. Toxin levels in the sediments were noticeably lower across most of the slough's reaches. Some of the lowest levels of pesticides and heavy metals were reported in Buffalo Slough. And PCBs in Buffalo sediments were virtually undetectable. Finally, there was real progress to celebrate. The most tenacious of slough toxins, bound up in the mud, releasing their grip at last.

My nightmares of getting mired in the mud have finally ceased. But would I ever sit on the shoreline and make mudpies with grandchildren? No way. Not in my lifetime. And probably not in theirs.

16 CITIZEN CROW: UP TO NO GOOD

The Crow God as depicted
In all of the reliable Crow bibles
Looks exactly like a Crow.
Damn, says Crow, this makes it
so much easier to worship myself.

SHERMAN ALEXIE, "CROW
TESTAMENT," *RESERVATION
BLUES*

I WAS DRIVING HOME with Miranda when something black plopped onto the windshield. We both jumped. It looked like a wet sack of trash—or a glob of rotting maple leaves. A mass of disheveled feathers appeared. Then a head. It was a small crow! A fledgling. It scrabbled for purchase on the slick windshield, finally clutching the wipers. Then it twisted around and glared at us through the glass.

"It's got blue eyes!" Miranda shouted. "Spooky. Like a White Walker!"

The baby crow also had a small pink streak at the corner of its mouth. Slowing the car, I looked for a place to pull off.

"You think those eyes are some kind of mutation?" I asked.

Our daughter whipped out her phone and filmed the bird. She looked worried. "In the movies, crows are a bad omen."

I recalled "Counting Crows," the children's poem. "One for sorrow, two for mirth . . ." In folktales, a crow could be a trickster, a weather forecaster, or a harbinger of death.

"It looks sick," I said. "Maybe it's starving."

"I'm posting this video," Miranda announced. "My friends will be amazed."

"Don't bring us bad luck."

The crow continued to glare.

We were on a busy residential street with no parking, so stopping was difficult. If this blue-eyed crow hitched a ride to our home, what then? Drop it off at the Audubon Society?

The crow stretched its wings and fluttered off our windshield onto the street. In the rearview mirror, I saw it hunkered down in the center lane. Oncoming traffic veered around it.

"It's gonna get squashed," cried Miranda.

"Crows don't squash easily," I said. "They're tough bastards."

Afterward, Miranda and I did some research and learned that crow fledglings all have blue eyes, which turn brown at maturity. This youngster likely toppled from its nest just as our car passed beneath.

At home on the slough, we interact with crows daily. Nancy and I call them "everywhere birds." In the early evening, they blacken the sky. When a crow shadow passes overhead like the scythe of the Grim Reaper, we duck reflexively. In our neighborhood, their numbers have exploded. The piles of garbage at nearby tent and RV camps make easy pickings. While a few crows might be company, hundreds are an invading army.

Crows eyeball us in the garden like tower guards tracking inmates in the prison yard. They scrutinize every spade of turned soil for high-value treats. Worms, grubs, beetles. They also bully other birds at the feeders and raid the compost barrel whenever I forget to shut the lid.

And they're not at all finicky about their food. Crows devour pizza with the same gusto they bring to a dead squirrel or Norway rat. An open garbage container offers five-star dining, but the crows around our house diversify their diets with spiders, beetles, grasshoppers, butterflies, garter snakes, walnuts, pet food, carrion. They especially crave cherries, fighting off the raccoons and starlings as soon as they ripen.

The American crow's scientific name, *Corvus brachyrhynchos,* sounds innocuous enough, translating as "raven with a short beak." But considering themselves the bosses of the neighborhood, they harass coyotes, dogs, raccoons, rabbits, nutrias, cats—and each other. They hang around our house in the trees and open meadows, where they eat, play, mate, and generally goof off, making an unpleasant racket that some ornithologists jokingly call "cawcophony."

Their harsh chorus often gets on my nerves. "Shut up!" I shout, as if they're inconsiderate neighbors having a raucous all-night party. But the crows just turn up the volume. Maybe they think that if it's too loud, I'm too old. I finally installed an outdoor brass bell. I ring it whenever the crows get out of hand. It silences them—but not for long. Fool me once, shame on you. Fool me twice . . .

For a variety of reasons, a group of these birds is known as a "murder." Since they always seem to be squabbling about something, I prefer a "kerfuffle of crows." Sometimes they tumble around in the wind, resembling a "cartwheel of crows."

Working in the garden, I have ample opportunity to observe them. And it's clear they observe me. Since we share common ground, I say hello to the ones in earshot. It's what neighbors do, even if they have their differences. "Good morning, Citizen Crow!" I greet them. "Snack on any tater tots today?" The sound of my voice seems to insult them. Some turn their backs. Others fly away.

I tried this joke on one. "What does a French crow sound like?" I asked. Silence. "PourCUAWWW! PourCUAWWW!" I shouted. The crow fled up into a cottonwood.

Addressing crows directly might be a serious faux pas. Perhaps they find it disrespectful, like a commoner getting overly chummy with royalty. I'm told crows hold grudges. If so, I'm in trouble for daring to joke around with my betters.

People consider crows pests, but they're crazy smart pests, always flaunting their high IQs. Close to our house, they crack walnuts, chestnuts, snails, and freshwater mussels onto pavement or rocks, repeatedly adjusting their drop heights until the shells shatter and release a feast of sweet meats. Sheer genius. They also snag golf balls. When dropped, they bounce down the street, and I have to suppress an urge to cry "FORE!" The crows are experts at snagging snacks off the patio dinner table too. From dense cover, two or three will silently size up the situation. Then one will strike when it's safe, seize a chicken bone or chunk of cheese, and flap off to safety, where it squabbles with its confederates over the prize.

Scientists confirm that crows never forget a face—and pass on this knowledge genetically to their offspring. They also claim crows can solve eight-step puzzles and bend twigs to fashion tools that enable them to scoop insects out of nooks and crannies. Crow researchers recently discovered that these everywhere birds think about their thinking. Masters of metacognition, a crucial component of human consciousness. "I think, therefore I am," declared Descartes, but crows need no French philosopher to validate proof of existence. One loud CAW! settles the matter.

Crows mate for life. Since the male has no penis, reproduction requires a vigorous round of aerial breakdancing. Above my house, a mating pair will fall pell-mell through the air, claws locked together, as if on a wild carnival ride, as they perform a butt-to-butt maneuver called a cloacal kiss. In mating season, males and females unleash a combo of non-caw sounds, including coos, rattles, and growls.

Though crows show no inclination toward organized religion, they apparently have a spiritual side. They gather around their deceased in great numbers, seeming to mourn. On the flip side, according to the University of Washington's ornithologist Kaeli Swift, crows sometimes have sex with their dead. Bird nerds call this "neCROWphilia."

During nesting season along the shores of the slough, the crows run super silent. A wide variety of birds nest in cedars, cottonwoods, willows, cattails, yellow flag irises, and slough grass. Nesting birds attract predators, especially crows.

A kill team of corvids will move through the canopy like Ninja assassins. The alarmed cries of adult robins, black-capped chickadees, nuthatches, or red-winged blackbirds follow. The parents try to defend their nests, but it's no contest. Crow attackers use superior size to sweep them aside and steal eggs or hatchlings. Beneath the trees, shattered eggshells appear. Once I saw a crow perched on a telephone wire, the limp body of a newborn bird dangling from its beak.

The Columbia Slough attracts other predatory birds—red-tailed and sharp-shinned hawks, bald eagles, ospreys, and more. Crows consider raptors an existential threat to the Worldwide Empire of Corvids. If a red-tailed hawk, on the lookout for rabbits and voles, perches high on a giant sequoia or cottonwood, crows scramble into action like fighter pilots intercepting an enemy aircraft. A sentry summons them to the correct coordinates. Then they congregate in the targeted tree to surround the hawk, unleashing a sonic storm of outrage.

At this point, the hawk either ignores its tormentors—or flies off. If the hawk takes flight, the crows pursue. Some closely tail the hawk. Others flank it, doing barrel rolls. A few attempt acrobatic landings on the hawk's back to peck its head and neck.

One afternoon a bald eagle flew fast over the water, trying to shake off a half dozen crows. Three red-winged blackbirds tailed the crows. A laugh line from large to small. In situations like this, small birds use superior maneuverability to torment the bigger ones.

Crows once had friends in high places. They served the gods. The Norse God Odin had two ravens (crows on steroids) as divine advisers—Hugin (thought) and Munin (memory). These cunning corvids kept an eye on the troublesome mortals. Just as they spy on us still, ever on the lookout for edible scraps.

One day on the Broadmoor Golf Course, a small bulldozer was excavating close to a sand trap. A water line had burst, flooding parts of the fairway, and scores of crows marched behind the bulldozer as it worked the earth.

Through binoculars, Nancy and I observed them. The crows were bowing their heads in unison. They looked like penitents in black robes come to confess their sins.

"What are they up to now?" Nancy asked.

"No good."

We watched the crows snatch up bits from the soaked dirt.

"They're eating goose poop!" Nancy laughed. "Wet goose poop. Ugh!"

It's easy to build a case against a bird that eats poop and whose squawking raises the dead. Still, as the children's song goes, "All God's creatures got a place in the choir." I just wish crows could carry a tune.

17 BIOACCUMULATION IS A BITCH

❝ **I know the human being and fish can coexist peacefully.**

GEORGE W. BUSH, POLITICAL SPEECH,
SAGINAW MICHIGAN

. . .

GROWING UP, I had the good fortune to live on lakes and rivers. My brother and I fished for bass and bream off an aluminum boat in rural South Carolina. We ate our catches, dredged in cornmeal, pan-fried in Crisco. Olive oil was an unknown. My brother and father fished for fun and for food. I fished only for food. This is why I'll never bait a hook and drop a line in the Buffalo Slough. But others do.

Daniel Pop was fishing the slough in 2012 when he landed a large sucker fish off Kelley Point. He'd often cast a line there since immigrating from Romania nineteen years earlier. That day, an environmental scientist from Columbia Riverkeeper approached him and offered to buy his sucker fish for testing. Pop readily agreed, adding that he and other fishers ignored the posted fish warning signs.

In an *Oregonian* interview Pop theorized that he and other immigrants fished the slough because they were used to muddy freshwater fish. "You want a taste that reminds you of your country," he said.

Alas, the taste of muddy water isn't all that comes with slough fish. Pop's sucker fish harbored PCB levels 270 times higher than the EPA recommendation for human consumption. High levels of PCBs appear in fish throughout the waterway. And fish are a big deal for those who care about the slough. They've even earned an ominous label: Primary Risk Pathway of Concern.

Eating fish from the slough is the main way humans can be harmed by toxins, now that splashing around in the water is not the summer pastime it was for the Gieses and their friends.

Carp and sucker fish are long-living omnivores—they nibble on algae and other plants; they gobble up insects, aquatic worms, crustaceans, and mollusks. These small animals, termed benthic (living along water bottoms), absorb toxins primarily through aquatic plants. Poisons that are bioavailable (absorbable by living things) migrate from plants to tiny animals to larger animals— often growing more concentrated as they move up the food chain.

Slough anglers like Daniel Pop are often low-income folks or recent immigrants who settled in the working-class neighborhoods of North and Northeast Portland. In recent years, I've seen fishing lines extending off some of the ramshackle boats that now cluster in and around the slough.

On a recent walk along the Peninsula Canal, Bruce and I noticed that the levee's fish warning signs had been updated. Bright orange, green, and yellow signs announcing WARNING in twelve languages had replaced the faded, bullet-pocked old ones. Online information warns anglers off eating resident fish, those species that spend their entire lives in the slough. Pesticides and PCBs are mentioned, along with the highlighted tip that CONTA-MINATED FISH DO NOT LOOK OR ACT SICK. Anglers are advised to throw away all bones, skin, and fat before cooking. Also, to avoid eating more than one fillet a month, especially if pregnant.

I can take a pass on eating slough fish, but I love to watch them in action. I hang my head off the dock to see minnows dart for shade under the willows. In our early years, when the clogged culvert dammed up a deeper pond, large carp spawned at the east end in late spring. We'd watch them leap, splash, and wallow in the reed grass and yellow flag iris, making a ruckus loud enough to bring me out of the house. This bucking behavior, I learned, disperses the carp eggs. Through our binoculars, none of these leaping giants appeared three-eyed or sore-pocked.

Like the sediment study, DEQ's most recent fish report, released in 2018, was a whopper, weighing in at over three thou-sand pages. I had to fill out a form to get that one, too. It analyzed samples from fifty-nine carp and suckers caught in 2015. Four fish from the Buffalo Slough made the study.

The highest pesticide concentrations among sampled fish showed up in an ancient carp from the Buffalo. The pesticide was chlordane, a compound of hydrogen and chlorine. For forty years (1948–88), chlordane was broadcast on food and other crops, sprayed in buildings and on lawns and gardens to kill insects. In humans, even moderate chlordane exposure causes headaches, nausea, vomiting, tremors, and mental confusion. High exposure brings convulsions and a heightened risk of liver cancer.

I had my own experience with chlordane. In college, I used the pesticide to kill large black ants that snaked along the baseboards of my rural home. The clear spray streaming from the pump smelled pungent and reedy, pleasantly antiseptic. But chlordane was overkill for my ant problem. My poor puzzle-solving skills I now attribute to that exposure.

Chlordane hangs around in soils and sediments—up to twenty years. And it holes up in fish fats. The Buffalo's chlordane carp was an estimated seventeen years old. Ironically, it is still legal to manufacture chlordane in the US, but only for export. An unsuspecting immigrant might serve up for dinner a chlordane-laced carp caught in the slough. In their home country, they might also have sprayed this poison to control termites.

Our country's environmental racism knows no borders. It's rampant everywhere—and quite visible in the placement of landfills, incinerators, and hazardous waste disposal units in low-income neighborhoods and/or communities of color. The positive correlation of race and income to pollutant exposure is well established in data on air pollution, proximity to Superfund sites, and inadequate systems for handling storm, waste, and drinking waters (think Flint, Michigan). Even today Alabama residents lacking sewer access and affordable septic tanks are forced to pipe their sewage overground from house to yard. One wonders what infrastructure even means in the US in the absence of basic supports for treating our wastes.

Two of the four fish caught in the Buffalo Slough made the top toxins hit list. A seven-year-old sucker fish bore the highest concentration of DDT of any slough samples. I scratched my head at this. A pesticide banned nearly fifty years ago showing up at high levels in a relatively young sucker fish. What gives?

Like many boomers, I raced my friends on childhood summer days in our small town, trying to catch the DDT spray truck as it rumbled down the hot asphalt, spewing poison out both sides. We flapped our arms and squawked like crows as we ran through drifting clouds of the deadly stuff.

DDT (dichloro-diphenyl-trichloroethane) was the first of the modern insecticides synthesized in the 1940s. Labeled a miracle weapon in the war against malaria, typhus, and other insect-borne human diseases, DDT was doused on crops and livestock, homes, and gardens. Marketing clips are still available on the internet, grainy black-and-white films showing summer camp children, laughing, and eating white bread sandwiches, while being sprayed with DDT.

"So safe you can eat it!" announces a deep male voice. And so, we did. Postwar kids trusted our government—until we grew up and didn't.

Thank the heavens for Rachel Carson and *Silent Spring.* As I puzzled over the persistence of DDT in the Buffalo Slough's seven-year-old sucker fish, I was reminded of a line from her 1962 masterpiece: "In nature, nothing exists alone."

DDT remained in use more than a decade after Carson publicized its toxicity to the world. By then, it had nearly wiped out our national bird and other raptors, whose intake of contaminated prey animals thinned the bird's eggshells and prevented hatching.

Humans also were sickened by DDT. Exposed to high levels, people shake, vomit, and suffer seizures. Concentrated in human fat, DDT has been linked to breast cancer, lymphoma, leukemia, and pancreatic cancer. And it lingers in the environment: Even now, fifty years after it was banned, DDT still shows up in human breast milk.

But pesticides weren't the lone villain in the study of Buffalo Slough fish. Among all the samples, Buffalo fish held the fifth highest accumulation of PCBs.

* * *

PCBS 101, A SIDE NOTE

Synthesized in 1929, PCBs were sold as miracle chemicals. They were nonflammable, insoluble in water, and chemically stable. They seemed virtually indestructible.

And, PCBs had so many uses. Adhering beautifully to glass and metal, they appeared in electrical insulation, paints, varnishes, adhesives, lacquers, proof paper, plasticizers, fireproofing cloth, ink, and lubrication. PCBs cooled, insulated, and coated machinery—and were added to dozens of everyday products—even chewing gum, to soften the bite.

By 1935, Monsanto controlled production in the US.

Early on, the skin of workers who handled PCBs erupted in disfiguring pustules. Soon after, many developed liver problems. As early as 1949, the dangers of PCBs were noted in a major industrial toxicology text: "Systemic poisoning from these chlorinated substances usually follows the inhalation of fumes. Damage is severe, and occasionally fatal. Acute yellow atrophy of the liver is . . . associated with serious exposure. . . Three fatalities were reported in 1936–37."

Nevertheless, Monsanto produced and sold the toxin for another forty years. Toxicity studies piled up, and they were consistent. People who handled the chemical suffered disfiguring skin diseases; many sickened and died.

Eventually, the EPA (Environmental Protection Agency) determined that PCBs caused cancer—primarily liver cancer and malignant melanomas—in animals. The poisons also wreaked havoc on the endocrine, reproductive and immune systems. Finally, in 1979, PCBs were taken off the market.

Even now, PCBs linger in our bodies as well as in materials made before the 1980s, in old transformers and capacitors, voltage regulators, motor and hydraulic systems oil, electrical appliances, fluorescent light ballasts, cable and thermal insulation, fiberglass, felt, foam, cork, adhesives, tape, floor finishes, and caulking.

* * *

I WAS surprised by the high levels of PCBs and pesticides in Buffalo fish. Though I complained about the shallow water and poor kayaking conditions, the widened culvert to Buffalo Slough enabled fish to swim in fresher water and pluck insects from cleaner sediments than in years past. Where did these toxic fish start out? How far did they range? And what did they eat to accumulate all these toxins?

Pondering these questions, I imagined the micro-journey of a PCB molecule. Let's call him PCB Pete. Pete was a midcentury molecule with a large extended family. He was birthed from four basic elements: carbon, hydrogen, chlorine, and oxygen. Pete's first cousins were the common pesticides made from chlorinated hydrocarbons, including DDT and chlordane. Let's say Pete was used to lubricate a crankshaft—perhaps the old crankshaft Bruce and I saw sticking out of the slough mud one late summer. Over the years, the crankshaft rusted, and Pete leaked out into the sediments. Pondweed roots soaked up Pete's more soluble PCB compounds. Midges and bottom-dwelling worms nibbled on these weeds. And then, our carp and sucker fish swallowed these worms and midges. At each successive meal, more PCB molecules joined Pete, and their numbers concentrated in fish tissues.

Fish live in water sullied by many sources. To settle dust, a growing postwar Portland sprayed PCB oils on roads that drained into the watershed. More PCBs spilled off trucks and boats and dumped engine, transformer, and car parts. Contaminated runoff flowed in from outfalls, stormwater, and groundwater.

Buffalo Slough's toxic fish may have swum in water already contaminated from the lower slough or from Whitaker Ponds nearby. But they also may have lived in our waters all their lives. Fish can concentrate toxins even from sediments that test clean. Bioaccumulation is a bitch.

Watching Gus dip for minnows at the waterline, I can't help but wonder what extra ingredients spike our heron's meal. I'm relieved to see no anglers casting a line on the Buffalo Slough. Still, for the sake of those who fish other reaches, maybe "fish safe to eat" is a worthy goal for a food source labeled a "primary pathway of concern." But safe-to-eat slough fish is not a dish I'm waiting for. Some of these poisons hang around forever.

18 WHAT GARDENS MAY COME

Soil is not just a substance, soil is the soul.

AMIT KALANTRI, *WEALTH OF WORDS*

· · ·

Dirt dribbled between my fingers. Billions of bacteria. Millions of fungal organisms. Microscopic masses of nematodes. Handfuls of earthworms. At my feet, a scurry of pill bugs, ants, millipedes, and springtails. A mini-verse of the seen and unseen gathered around a dead dog named Sadie. The whole gang there to welcome her back home and rearrange her complex molecules of fat, blood, and bone into fertile soil.

In *The Devil's Dictionary*, Ambrose Bierce railed against any kind of burial that didn't convert a corpse into compost ASAP, stating that the dead person should be "ornamenting his neighbor's lawn as a tree or enriching his table as a bunch of radishes." He added that "the violet and the rose are languishing for a nibble at his gluteus maximus."

Sadie was our white shepherd lab, our boon companion. For sixteen years, she swam lakes and climbed mountains with us. Even in death she was part of our family. So, wanting to keep her close, we wrapped her body in a blue cotton blanket and lowered her into the ground in the southwest corner of our property, surrendering her lovely bones to the hungry earth.

Sadie had been failing for weeks. She couldn't eat, drink, or sleep well. It was summer 2009, and it was too hot for her inside the house. I was in southern Oregon on a camping trip, but Nancy and Miranda curled up on either side of her as she slept on the cooling concrete driveway. In the distance, a pack of coyotes yipped. Sadie groaned and panted. Nancy cupped water in her hand, urging Sadie to drink, but she wouldn't. She died the next evening.

If all dogs go to heaven, the journey there goes through the soil. Sadie's body would decay into a spongy mass of organic matter, the relentless invasions of minerals, microorganisms, acids, and water transforming her tissues into phosphorus and potassium. Calcium, magnesium, sulfur. Clay, sand, humus. Fingers of dark earth would unravel her mortal coil and unleash her spirit, freeing her to bound back to the beginning of things.

Sadie's death reminded me how soil softens the hardness of the world. Hardwood and hard hearts. It all gets pulled back into the ground, a process where shape becomes shapeless. Giving life and taking life, soil nourishes all the plant and animal kingdoms. Grass grows, gazelles graze on its life-giving green, but every organism caught up in the spin cycle of creation must ultimately meet its maker. From the alphabet of death, soil spells out the story of each life down to the final syllable. It keeps us close. It hides beneath our fingernails, discolors our skins, coats our tongues, clings to our lungs, and eats us dead or alive.

The soil that cradles life on our planet has only been around about 450 million years. Takes a long time for lichen to chew rock into a teaspoon of grit. Even longer for horsetails, clubmosses, and native grasses to chemically convert this raw material into fertile soil, a biodynamic breadbasket for the billions. On average, it takes a full century to generate a stingy inch of topsoil. The accretion of enough soil to grow wheat takes roughly three millennia. Historically, humans have displayed a dangerous disregard for soil conservation, wasting the wealth of the land through greed, ignorance, and incompetence. "The nation that destroys its soil destroys itself," Franklin D. Roosevelt warned.

Eager to garden without chemicals, Nancy and I began to pay attention to soil after moving to the slough. Walking our property in those early days, we searched out the best locations for fruits and vegetables. A soil test kit indicated a 6–6.5 pH range. This meant good garden growing. The phosphorous, potassium, calcium, and magnesium levels also checked out. In retrospect, I deeply regret not holding some soil in my hand and crumbling it. I failed to check for friability. A boneheaded mistake. Friable soil promotes root health and creates what's called a "Goldilocks zone" where water doesn't drain off too fast or too slowly.

Because the golf course next door used herbicides and synthetic fertilizers, we were relieved that a test of well water showed somewhat elevated nitrate levels, but still below the 10 mg/l standard. No PCBs or heavy metals either. The water wouldn't kill us, or our plants.

To learn more about living dirt, I read about the natural history of the Columbia Slough. Before the era of dams, dikes, levees, and drainage canals, our local watershed had experienced frequent flooding, including the successive catastrophic Missoula

Floods that reamed out the Columbia River Basin approximately fifteen thousand years ago. The river had shifted course many times, creating vast wetlands and broad alluvial fans of sand and gravel. To my thinking, flooding meant fertility. Ancient agrarian civilizations along the Tigris-Euphrates and the Nile depended on floods to regenerate the land. I assumed the Columbia River had done likewise, enriching our property with thousands of years of sand, volcanic ash, loess, and other beneficial sediments that would turn any garden into a breadbasket. More than enough to feed us and our neighbors.

Ready to launch an urban garden, I sank a shovel into the soil —and three inches down, hit hard gray clay. The fertility of our property was skin deep. More than a century of commercial development had scraped the land clean of nutrient-rich native soil and vegetation, leaving behind a hardpan of clay. I wanted to know what I was contending with, so I performed a simple test using the standard Mason jar technique. I added the prescribed amount of water and dish soap to a soil sample, then gave everything a vigorous shake until the contents became a chocolate-colored slurry. I did the same for other locations around the yard, leaving each jar undisturbed for several days. They all produced the same result: The water stayed muddy while a thin sedimentary layer of sand and other particles collected at the bottom. This confirmed that our soil was predominately clay. Water wouldn't drain quickly. When wet soil clung to my boots, it weighed me down like ten-pound weights strapped to my ankles. Dry, the clay hardened like concrete. Not good for growing carrots.

"Maybe we could mold pots from it," Nancy joked.

"And sell them as bird bidets," I added.

Clay has some good qualities. It's packed with beneficial silicon, iron, magnesium, and alkaline compounds. Unfortunately, clay also captures pesticide, herbicide, heavy metal, and synthetic fertilizer residues. A big problem. Coneflowers, bee balm, and joe-pye weed tolerate almost any kind of clay, but broccoli and snap peas need friable soil that circulates water and nutrients effectively. Best of all, proper garden soil wicks away suspect substances.

I was determined to improve my soil without relying on the

short-sighted sorcery of modern chemistry. Using fossil fuel fertilizers was like starting a fire with kerosene instead of kindling. A slow and steady fire was better than a flash-in-the pan whoosh. We couldn't grow plants without first growing the soil. Houses are built from the foundation up—not from the roof down.

We got busy right away, laying cardboard over all but a strip of lawn, adding many cubic yards of compost, chicken manure, straw, and wood chips on top. I hoped to encourage earthworms, insects, and bacteria to break the clay down into humus. To promote nitrogen fixation, I planted cover crops like red crimson clover and fava beans. I also made my own biochar from hardwood lump charcoal. Among its other benefits, biochar helps stop nutrient leaching from soil during watering or heavy rains. Biochar is made much like charcoal, but the trick to making it correctly requires a burning process that uses a minimum of oxygen. I covered my coals with dirt and let them smolder like a peat moss fire. Results were mixed but using DIY biochar was better than paying top dollar for it at a nursery.

Our first spring harvest was spectacular. Wowie-zowie! Everything we planted flourished. Spinach, kale, cabbage, broccoli, peas, parsley, lettuce, mustard, arugula, collards, and pak choi. The vigor of the plants impressed Willow, my older daughter.

"Your spinach is dinosaur-sized," she said.

By the next growing season, the bugs had found us. Our vegetable starts suffered severe predation from the usual suspects. Aphids, thrips, red spider mites, cutworms, cabbage moths, scale, grubs, slugs, etc.

"Where are all the aphid-eating ladybugs?" I kept asking Nancy. "And why aren't the birds helping us out more?"

"Bugs don't have to work for a living here." She was thumbing gray aphids off the cauliflower.

Each day, Nancy took stock of the damage, scowling at me through eyeholes bird-pecked into the spinach, chard, and kale leaves. Lots of hanging chard. And then she stepped in a mole hole, twisted her ankle, and developed a bad limp.

"This isn't a good look in nature," she grumbled. "The coyotes will think I'm easy pickings."

One afternoon, I saw something that seemed like another bad omen. A lone vole appeared, weaving shakily through rows of green beans. A gray film clouded its dark eyes. Had it been poisoned? A couple of scrub jays arrived on the scene and attacked, pecking the vole's head and little round ears furiously. I drove off the birds, but the vole died, and I buried it nearby. I felt a little spooked. Had my garden somehow killed it? Maybe I'd used too much blood meal.

We launched a counterattack on the bad bugs with a full arsenal of organic pesticides. Neem oil, insecticidal soap, BT *(Bacillus thuringiensis)*, horticultural oil, pyrethrin, sulfur, and red pepper sprays. We gave the little buggers the works but achieved only sketchy success. Our garden survived the insect invasion, but never again looked as good as that first spring.

This was in due in part to birds, who also laid claim to the fruit of our labors. Goldfinches pecked holes through the sunflower leaves until the stems stood naked. We'd planted a dozen blueberry bushes, and at harvest time, the robins, starlings, and cedar waxwings got first pickings. Crows stripped clean our cherry tree. Apple maggots and codling moths attacked the Honeycrisp apples, and the black-headed juncos finished the job, using their beaks to break apart the fruity flesh with the force of a jackhammer.

The moles, of course, never let up. The enriched soil spawned an abundance of red wigglers *(Eisenia fetida.)* The moles gorged themselves on these worms. Huge mounds erupted throughout the garden, toppling tomato plants, and overturning sturdy rows of broccoli. Despite our losses, overplanting left us plenty.

Growing food has always been hard on the body. Exhausted from the stoop labor of planting and weeding, I often take a break and stretch out flat, aligning my backbone with the earth. Daylight or dark. Dawn or dusk. Anytime is good to cozy up to the songbirds, stinkbugs, spiders, damselflies.

Home gardening and broadscale farming also take a toll on the natural environment. Our planet was probably happier when *Homo sapiens* survived through hunting and gathering. Barring a global reversal in business as usual, we're not likely to return to the Stone

Age simplicity of eating grasshoppers, mealworms, roots, seeds, and berries.

The illusory comforts of industrialized food production beguile us into a sense of security, alienating us from the fundamentals of growing our own. More than local farmers, supermarkets and fast-food chains fill our bellies, often with over-processed food denuded of nutrients. A world of eight billion people is a hungry world.

Sadly, extracting food from exhausted land is a zero-sum proposition. We labor to wring wealth from weary fields, using fossil fuel fertilizers to tease out another crop of gene-tweaked soybeans. Cattle ranchers overgraze public lands, corporate farmers drain Ice Age aquifers, and Big Ag uses GMO gimcrackery to grow Frankenfood. In this all-out war on the soil, nobody wins. Wendell Berry, who regarded soil as a national treasure, lays it out plainly: "Without proper care for it, we can have no community, because without proper care for it we can have no life."

Quick solutions don't exist, but it's clear that more people need to learn to grow more of their own food. Teaching sustainable gardening/farming as a basic skill in the K-12 curriculum would be a crucial first step, revolutionizing our relationship with the land, and bringing humans into closer compliance with the natural laws of the planet.

Natural law also instructs us on how to dispose of our dead in an earth-friendly manner. To regenerate both flesh and spirit, the Mayans buried the dead with corn seeds in their mouths, wrapping the bodies in cotton cloth. A friend of mine yearns to "be a tree," something he picked up from reading Old English folklore. If he's buried with an acorn in his mouth, his afterlife will assume the shape of a mighty oak. I'd prefer a biodegradable burial shroud. One with pockets full of wildflower seeds. Plant me and I will grow goldenrod, foxgloves, bee balm, and tidy tips.

Right now, Sadie lies beneath my shoulder blades, a muddle of bones, stones, thistle seeds, dandelion roots, and worm castings. Ghostly filaments of mycorrhizal fungi have wrapped up her disaggregated self, branching out like the neural networks of human brains as they ingest sugar, fix nitrogen, and deliver phosphorous to the plant kingdom.

I grow a garden because it feeds us, but I also derive deep satisfaction from seeing how each seed springs from the soil in its joyous jump from darkness to sunlight. Soil is both world maker and undertaker, incorporating what poet Dylan Thomas named "the force that through the green fuse drives the flower."

At some point, the green fuse fizzles out. We die and go to ground, spilling willy-nilly like loose change from a torn pocket. Eventually the soil claims it all, to grow what gardens may come.

19 GREENS TO ROUGH

> **Although golf was originally restricted to wealthy, overweight Protestants, today it's open to anybody who owns hideous clothing.**

DAVE BERRY, *STAY FIT AND HEALTHY UNTIL YOU'RE DEAD*

. . .

One week after Oregon's governor issued our first COVID statewide stay-at-home order, a fat first-class packet arrived from the US Army Corps of Engineers. Postmarked March 27, 2020, it was a Public Notice of Permit Application. Ripping it open, I felt my chest tighten. Regular people only get these mailings when someone wants to mess with your neighborhood. Inside were nineteen paper-clipped pages and twelve maps. Before I'd read a single line, I knew Broadmoor Golf Course had sold at last.

Living beside the golf course was like having an annoying cousin holed up next door. Sometimes he hosts loud parties for obnoxious friends who hurl beer cans over the fence. Other times, he brings over a six-pack and makes you laugh. He grates on your nerves, but you've learned to tolerate him. On occasion he's an albatross around your neck, but he's family.

And now we'd have a new neighbor. Prologis, Inc., seemed an unlikely buyer. A multi-billion-dollar logistics firm with properties all over the world, Prologis builds large warehouses and distribution hubs that sprawl over a hundred acres or more, with dozens of truck bays transporting tons of cargo in and out. The city had rezoned only fifteen acres next to us for industrial use. The rest of the golf course, 100+ acres, remained Open Space, protected from development by the three major slough reaches transecting it. A mere fifteen industrial acres offered much less real estate than Prologis buildings typically span.

At age ninety, Broadmoor was one of Portland's oldest public courses. It opened in 1931, when six sisters bought a dairy farm and converted 170 acres of Columbia River floodplain into a golf course. Their family home, an ornate two-story Victorian with gingerbread cutouts and slanted bay windows, perched high on Columbia Blvd. next to the clubhouse and tenth tee. That original house was long gone. The golf course, though, stayed in the family and was now managed by a great-nephew named Scott.

Like the Giese girls, Bruce and I collected golf balls on Broadmoor walks at dusk. Many lay inside the blackberry brambles or nestled in muddy roughs. I rubbed off caked-on dirt before dumping them into a hand-painted Turkish bowl to give to our friend Dale. Because he occasionally lost balls when golfing the Broadmoor, he'd inspect each one for his own unique tag.

We weren't the only ball collectors. In good weather, a wiry retired teacher often paddled up the Buffalo in a stubby orange kayak. Driving his prow into yellow flag iris, he'd slog out in hip boots onto the northern slope to comb through the vegetation for balls. One day he saw me reading on the dock.

"Wife says this gets me out of the house!" he shouted through cupped hands. "I just give the balls away!"

"So do we!" I yelled back.

Broadmoor looked shabby compared to the private members-only golf courses nearby. The asphalt had buckled on many cart paths. Potholes collected water and sprouted thorny thistles and teasels. Sheets of plywood covered a hole over the main slough bridge, made from a Burlington Northern railroad trestle. Cigar-like tubes of black-and-white goose poop remained on the greens for days, awaiting the hard-working but understaffed ground crew and their gas-powered blowers.

But Broadmoor had a wild beauty lacking in the city's mani-cured courses. The sisters lined the fairways with massive trees, rows and rows of giant sequoias, Douglas firs, western red cedars, and ponderosa pines. Huge cottonwoods, black locusts, birches, and willows grew old in the wetland slumps and roughs. Their porous wood ideal for nesting birds, they rotted, splintered, and collapsed after heavy winds and rain.

Three tongues of the slough meandered through the course: the wide and shallow Buffalo Slough, with our home on its southern shore; the main slough, a few hundred yards north of the Buffalo; and the mile-long Elrod Canal, a skinny channel that snaked west beside the Oregon Food Bank. Several side channels, some seasonal, also threaded the course. Beavers dammed narrow side streams and felled birch saplings across them.

Walking the golf course, we'd taken home more than golf balls. In the bordering woods, Bruce clipped dogwood stalks to plant on the nutria slides next to our house. At dusk one night, we caught the rare sight of a low-slung quadruped, likely a mink or stoat, humping fast like a hopped-up inchworm toward the safety of the

Elrod Canal. In the spring, careening red-tailed hawk mates claimed the northern cedars, coyotes scouted our movements, and bats darted through the insect columns that rose into warm air.

When Leona Giese moved away in her early nineties, she sold her home to a devout Christian couple who added ramps and remodeled the main bathroom for their wheelchair-using daughter. We bought it from these second owners, Allen and Sally.

When the four of us walked the property together before the closing, Sally, a slender woman with tight curls of graying hair, warned us about living next to the Broadmoor.

"If bad language offends you, beware! When some of these golfers make a bad shot, you'll want to cover your ears!"

Foul language was the least of our worries. And it turned out that Broadmoor Golf Course wasn't a bad neighbor, considering the potential hazards. Over a dozen years, we counted only a handful of direct ball strikes. There was the cracked west-side solar panel (free replacement). One tenth hole chip shot cracked a dining room window ($400). Three direct strikes on Bruce while gardening, one on the head, one on each shoulder. No visible injuries. Another errant shot shattered an old window we'd scavenged for insulating tender spring greens (outside weeding, I ducked, thinking rifle shot). Finally, a golf ball struck our new SUV, leaving a fist-sized dent (as of this writing, still not fixed).

In good weather, the groundskeepers hit the course before dawn in head-lit carts and tractors to mow, blow, and set sprinklers before the early birds arrived ($18, 18 holes, before 8:00 a.m.) Since we were also early risers, we could tune out the roar and whine of equipment. But our summer guests stumbled out bleary-eyed to their coffee, grumbling about lost sleep. For overnight stays, Miranda brought earplugs, eyebags, and turned a fan on high.

On the plus side, the groundskeepers often pulled over to chat, offering Bruce spare sand and mulch for our garden.

We always relished the rare days when the golf course was vacant. Atypical snowstorms closed it down, drawing neighbors to sled the steep slope at the tenth tee. During hard freezes, our dogs skidded wild-eyed over the frozen Elrod Canal. Windstorms also brought golfing to a halt when large cottonwood limbs crashed down. A couple of giant sequoias, massive cones heavy with needles, toppled over, leaving dirt-packed root balls upended above deep cavities. Several days later, the groundskeepers arrived to chainsaw the trunks and haul away the debris.

In spring of 2020, Broadmoor closed only a few weeks for COVID. Staff used the time to adapt the clubhouse restaurant for takeout and create social-distancing protocols. For a time, golf carts were grounded. Before golfing was rebranded as a safe way to socialize with friends, we were able to walk freely across the fairway bridges spanning the sloughs to reach the Catkin Marsh Natural Area at the northwest border. A nature reserve, Catkin's fifty-four acres of wildlife habitat was maintained by Portland Bureau of Environmental Services. Near its perimeter—not far from the Oregon Food Bank—we found the chorus of tree frogs deafening. On my phone, I recorded audio to send to a friend who lives at ten thousand feet in the Ecuadorian Andes. She sent back a recording of high mountain birdsong.

Like most golf courses these days, the Broadmoor hadn't made much profit. More than once, the family owners tried to rezone and sell the property for industrial use. We wrote letters, organized neighbors, and testified at city council meetings to fight plans that would remove or shrink the conservation zones.

Environmental Protection (EP) zones hugged the three slough reaches that cross the course. To protect wetlands and wildlife corridors, EP zones strictly prohibit new commercial and residential development. And the golf course had been identified as a critical stopover for migrating birds and at-risk bat species.

The city's 2010 Natural Resources Inventory stated: "The bats utilize water bodies for drinking and foraging and the trees for roosting, both day and night . . . Golf courses, particularly riparian corridors with tree canopy, are utilized by a high concentration and diversity of migratory birds as they travel along the Pacific Flyway, Columbia River, and Columbia Slough corridor. Willow flycatchers, an at-risk species, were documented on the east side of the Broadmoor."

Other factors complicated the golf course sale for industrial use. No roads transected its hundred-plus acres, which also abutted the Portland International Airport. For security and safety reasons, the Federal Aviation Authority limits the height of buildings in flyover zones.

Despite all these constraints, the City of Portland eventually did rezone fifteen acres of the golf course from Open Space to Industrial (IG2). With easy truck and rail access, this spot fronted Columbia Blvd. at the top of the historic floodplain. Rezoning furthered state goals to host more industry within city limits. More industry brings higher-wage jobs was the city's sound bite. I wondered how all the new self-storage facilities strung along Columbia Blvd. furthered this "jobs" goal—businesses that sell only locked-down space, staffed by a handful of low-wage employees.

With this partial rezoning, the Broadmoor Golf Course sale became more feasible. Unfortunately for us, those fifteen new industrial acres adjoined our property. Our NIMBY (Not in My Backyard) reactions were swift and predictable.

A few weeks later, a second first-class mailing arrived, describing an additional Prologis project a few miles west of us at Portland Meadows. A sprawling horse-racing track near the lower slough, Portland Meadows opened in 1945, entertaining families and bettors until it closed in 2015. The old horse track, wooden stables, and spectator stands were being razed to construct three Prologis buildings, which would span over a million square feet.

Like Broadmoor, Portland Meadows was built on the historic flood plain of the Columbia River. Scattered wetlands remained throughout. And wetlands—specifically, non-tidal, palustrine wetlands—provided the link between Prologis, Portland Meadows, and the Broadmoor.

These kinds of marshes once dominated the Columbia flood-plain but were now a diminished and disconnected scatter of seasonal wet spots. Freshwater wetlands recharge groundwater and moderate streamflow, helping protect against both floods and drought. Now concrete and asphalt smother many of these urban wetlands.

Like a sponge, watershed marshes reduce flood damage by slowing down and storing flood waters. As water moves through a marsh, sediments and other pollutants settle to the marsh floor. There, vegetation and microorganisms take up excess nutrients like nitrogen and phosphorus fertilizers that might otherwise pollute surface water. Mineral-rich soils of sand, silt, and clay lie below. Cattails, reeds, and bulrushes provide habitat for waterfowl and small mammals.

To build a massive logistics hub at Portland Meadows, Prologis would have to fill (i.e., destroy) seven acres of wetlands on the former racetrack's property. Deemed low value based on their degraded habitat and isolation from connecting water sources, those few acres of wetlands were nevertheless protected by Section 404 of the Clean Water Act.

This law, passed in 1972 by the Nixon administration, required developers to mitigate the loss of wetlands in one area by creating compensatory wetlands elsewhere in the same watershed. This exchange is called wetland mitigation banking. On first read, I thought "wetlands banking" referred to the mudbanks of the slough, but this is banking as in making deposits and withdrawals —environmental transactions a bit akin to cap-and-trade carbon offsets.

So Prologis bought the Broadmoor Golf Course not simply to build another warehouse, but to earn valuable credits by creating new wetlands in low-lying portions of the golf course. I reread that paragraph twice before I flew outside to find Bruce.

I found him on the south slope of the Buffalo, planting oak and pine saplings on the steep bank. The groundskeepers had tipped him off about the impending sale, so he'd gone into overdrive, planting saplings and shrubs to curb erosion caused by nutria slides. The golfers would soon be gone, he reasoned; in the meantime, the new plantings wouldn't block shots across the slough.

Over the years, walking the golf course at night, we'd often played "What If?" What would it look like if the manicured greens returned to a natural state? What if the sand traps filled with water, cattails, and spring symphonies of frogs? What if deer herds nested in new native shrubs and grasses? What if the coyotes made their dens close? Would they help cull the moles and nutria? Our imaginings, answers to the questions, felt like pipe dreams.

Prologis planned to dig deep trenches at the golf course's north end, a natural low spot near the Catkin Marsh. Their wetlands scientists had drilled feasibility bore wells to find the water table. By their reckoning, hitting water between ten and eleven feet required removing 195,000 cubic yards of soil. The new wetlands, spanning thirteen acres, would not be permanent ponds, which attract waterfowl that pose danger to air traffic. (The Port of Portland insisted on this.) Instead, Broadmoor's new wetlands would mimic those of the Catkin Marsh, water-saturated ground prevailing during wet months only.

Like most things involving the slough, trade-offs abounded. The plan called for excavated soil to be "disposed of" on the uplands at the southern end of the course. Our home bordered the designated dump zone; spreading that much new soil on the steep southern slough slope could spell trouble for local wildlife, sediments, and water. Bats, birds, and mammals nested in the large cottonwoods there.

I raised this with the wetlands scientist hired to oversee the Broadmoor's environmental assessment. John van Staveren, president of Pacific Habitat Services, had made time for a phone chat.

"We'll conduct an environmental review of the land beside you next," he said, in a lilting English accent. "Then another plan will follow for public comment."

Squinting at the map, I surmised a few details. A seventy-foot-tall earthen wall would be built and backfilled, leveling the steep slope up to Columbia Blvd. Atop the new flat pad would spread a large parking lot and a 268,000-square-foot warehouse. Along with dozens of other trees, the row of giant silver maples lining the slope would be chainsawed and hauled off. The new earthen wall would span a half mile east-west, partially obscuring the winter view of Mount Hood. To safely withstand the heavy truck traffic needed to move hundreds of loads of earth, the eastern bridges crossing the sloughs would be reinforced with temporary steel bridges.

We were worried. The Columbia corridor was Portland's priority spot for new industry. Migratory birds, wetlands, concrete, and asphalt don't mix well. The slough was still struggling back from a century of environmental wounds. More industrial development wouldn't give it the needed break.

At the same time, we were cautiously optimistic. The disruption of trucks beeping in and out seemed a fair trade for the return of 100+ acres to wetlands and meadows. And the plan called for new easements extending the Columbia Slough trail west across the former golf course. A new trail would enable neighbors from the "city" side of Columbia Blvd.—the Concordia, Woodlawn, and Cully neighborhoods—to enjoy the slough's wildlife.

"I just hope we live long enough to see some of this," I said to Bruce. "These projects take forever."

John van Staveren agreed. It would take years to transform the golf course into a proper nature park.

I gazed across the Buffalo Slough at the giant sequoias we'd planted a decade before. They now towered over forty feet, almost entirely blocking the ugly chain-link fence and power plant. I walked out to Bruce, who was planting more tiny saplings along the Buffalo. We pondered the vision for a future Broadmoor Park.

"We just need to keep planting trees," he said, bent to the task.

I nodded and picked up a shovel to help.

20 STANDING ON THE SKY BRIDGE

> **The easiest way to leave this world without leaving this world is to stand in the middle of the bridge and watch the surroundings.**

MEHMET MURAT ILDAN IN *STORIES THAT BRIDGE* BY VIVEK BHUSHAN SOOD

. . .

Heavy traffic to the left, a thirty-foot drop to the right. A truck engine growls, gears grinding, exhaust pipes belching diesel smoke. Below me, the tail end of a Union Pacific train rumbles westward, hauling tanks of crude oil for foreign export. Electric-yellow graffiti glares from one car. "Lost Angel." Then a blob of pink bubble script appears. "Get out Get out Get out."

I stop on the NE 33rd overpass that curves above Lombard and Columbia. Taking in a view of the Sunderland neighborhood, I clutch the low aluminum railing, my feet planted on a narrow, six-inch walkway. A dangerous spot to stand. Psychiatry has a name for fear of bridges: gephyrophobia. I suffer more from motorphobia, the fear of traffic.

Vehicles whoosh past. One driver negotiates the tight curve, her eyes cast down. She's texting. Walking across this overpass is a close encounter between bones and bumpers. Nancy agrees.

"A truck or bus could whack you," she says.

"It's the safest way to walk to the store," I counter.

"Susan drove past you the other day. She said you were just standing there. She wondered if you'd had a stroke."

Susan was a neighbor. Always making jokes. "I was just enjoying the view."

"Okay, but don't stop and stare. Please. A moving target is harder to hit."

This maintenance-deferred overpass offers treacherous passage for pedestrians and bicyclists, but to me it's a sky bridge. A grandiose name for such a sorry-looking structure, yet the highest section of the overpass levitates me between sky and earth, enabling me to take in the grassy green sweep of the Columbia River floodplain. On clear evenings, I have a ringside seat to the spectacular alpenglow of Mount Hood to the east and Mount St. Helens to the north. On particularly clear days, Mount Adams as well.

This sky bridge is also my personal panopticon, where I can cast an all-seeing eye on the round-the-clock commotion of the neighborhood. Lots of heavy-metal noise here. Screeching, thumping, banging. Trucks, cars, and motorcycles race freeway-fast along Columbia Blvd. Businesses belly up to greasy curbs, offering a wide assortment of industrial-strength sales and services.

From my perch, I see a couple of abandoned houses that look like the remains of scuttled fishing scows exposed by the outgoing tide. They crumble next to Columbia Blvd., their clapboards peeling. Blackberries and English ivy engulf rooftops. Starlings roost in the slump and crumble of chimneys.

Several people live in one of these maintenance-deferred houses. I see a young man in the front yard. Wearing a football jersey, sweatpants, and no shoes, he sits in a desk chair, head nodding. He seems unaware of the traffic racing past him. Nancy and I have seen him before. In the chair. Head nodding slowly. Over and over. We said hello once, but he didn't answer.

"Meth head," I said.

Nancy shook her head. "Nope, opiod."

"You sure?"

"Yep. Meth heads don't nod."

From the overpass, I can also see an encampment of a dozen or more people where NE 33rd Drive merges with Columbia Blvd. A fringe community of tents, vehicles, and wood shacks. A young woman and two toddlers climb from a battered hearse and join others around an open campfire.

Twenty blocks west from where I stand, a nursery sits among a scrabble of industrial shops. I buy vegetable starts, flowers, and perennial grasses there. The owner, Ernie, a man in his nineties who recently passed, had told me his father started the business during the Great Depression. Back then, Japanese American farmers grew their produce next to the Columbia Slough, using horse-drawn wagons to deliver fruits and vegetables.

"My mother bought cabbages, plums, and cucumbers from the Japanese," Ernie said. "Then World War II happened, and the government rounded them up. They lost everything."

Right now, the late afternoon sky shows cornflower blue with faint filaments of gray. The airport's air cannons erupt to chase off the geese, a series of closely syncopated detonations that sound like corks popped from supersized champagne bottles. First a pop, then a boom. *Poppa-boom, poppa-boom.* A great honking mob of Canada geese blackens the horizon. The big birds fly first in a clockwise circle, then go counterclockwise before twisting together into a tight knot and dropping from sight.

As if in chorus, the quacking of ducks follows from the side channels of the slough. Some are full-throated guffaws. *Ark! Ark! Ark!* Is there such a thing as Groucho Marx ducks? From the sound of it, these imitators deliver comedy lines from *A Night at the Opera*. I hear them above the din of traffic. *Your eyes, your throat, your lips! Everything about you reminds me of you. Except you. Ark! Ark! Ark!*

I recently watched buffleheads on the Columbia Slough. These little ducks gathered a few feet from where canary grass and black-berries hackled the mushy shoreline. Foraging for damselfly larvae, mud snails, and curly-leaf pondweed, they dove and popped back up. The males had eye-catching green and purple-colored heads. A few ducks ventured further from shore, the water the gray of a tarnished nickel.

Abruptly, a bald eagle swooped in from the south, the sun at its back. In unison, the buffleheads disappeared underwater. Synchronized ducking. The eagle circled back and hovered overhead, powerful wings agitating the water like helicopter blades, but the buffleheads stayed submerged. The massive bird finally gave up and perched on a utility pole, looking bedraggled. The ducks bobbed back into sight.

From my sky bridge, I survey the dishevelment of the former Broadmoor Golf Course, closed six months before. The boarded-up clubhouse still stands, but a few hundred yards to the northeast, steam shovels knock over giant sequoias and dig a network of drainage ditches to prepare for the upcoming construction.

The sight of so many uprooted giant sequoias appalls me. Many are nearly a hundred years old. I recall words from *FernGully: The Last Rainforest*. In this animated film, the Batty Koda character says: "First thing, all these trees go. Then come your highways, then come your shopping malls, and your parking lots, and your convenience stores."

Prologis aims to strike a balance between competing interests to bring a kinder, gentler form of industrial development. Native trees, shrubs, and grasses will support wetland wildlife. Mammoth warehouses, trucks, and parking lots support the human economy. It's like working out an algebraic equation, where what you do to one side, you must do equally to the other. All the variables should factor out, but nature uses its own math to calculate long-term costs. Costs to water, soil, and air bring into play the Second Law of Thermodynamics, which states that all order tends toward disorder, the condition called entropy. Usable energy degrades into unusable energy. Things go from hot to cold. Sci-fi writer Andy Weir says: "All my brilliant plans foiled by thermodynamics. Damn you, Entropy!"

Right now, the Broadmoor is a Rube Goldberg confoundment of downed trees, mud and moving machine parts metamorphizing eventually to new creations of concrete, steel, and asphalt. And all the fixings of a nature park. Closing my eyes, I imagine the thousands of native plants and tree to be planted around an eco-friendly kingdom of bioengineered bioswales and wetlands abuzz with migrating wildlife. Hopefully, the hard-charging poohbahs of economic progress agree with Thoreau's opinion that "We can never have enough of Nature."

Turning my gaze away from the Broadmoor, I look north over the floodplain, a vast geographic goulash of waterways, wetlands, levees, dikes, roads, commerce, industry, and dwellings. Beneath its surface, it sequesters a subterranean time machine, one that embeds the records of earthquakes, floods, volcanoes. Glaciers and megafauna. Native Americans, fur trappers, and wagon trains. Farms, factories, and old growth forests.

Though parts of the floodplain double as a public dump now, that despoilment pales before the huge (often-out-of-sight) mess the forces of nature have left behind. Right now, our neck of the Pacific Northwest may seem a peaceable kingdom, a mossy damp spot on the map where bicyclers and boaters coexist with birds, beavers, and blue-green algae. But this is an illusion. Mother Nature still holds weapons of mass destruction in her arsenal.

In the past, she packed her violence into the space of a few million years, selecting specific epochs to go stark raving mad and wipe out our part of the world with floods, volcanoes, and earthquakes. She smashed the furniture and brought down the house.

Regional Ragnaröks sliced, diced, and iced the terrain. Plate tectonics played bumper cars with mountain ranges. Volcanoes melted rock into boiling oceans of brimstone. Massive glaciers and catastrophic floods pulverized the earth.

Assorted animals survived these onslaughts, each clinging to its mayfly moment to shout its story, sing its song, dance its dance. Camels, crocodiles, hippos. Also, short-faced bears, dire wolves, woolly mammoths, saber-tooth cats. Even seven-foot beavers. Like graffiti, their fossilized bones tell us that "Kilroy was here."

The Anthropocene Age of Climate Change has arrived faster than we expected, shocking us like a mass shooter in the school-yard. Climate change won't spare the Pacific Northwest. In fact, it's already here. Wildfires, droughts, floods, pandemics. All the nasty stuff of a disaster film. And we're only a volcanic eruption or earthquake away from going full Ozymandias, approaching perilously close to "that colossal wreck, boundless and bare," described by Shelley.

If I had access to a user-friendly time machine, I'd dial up 1805 and watch Lewis and Clark paddling pirogues and dugout canoes beneath my sky bridge on their way to the Pacific Ocean. The explorers would find no industrial warehouses—just an aston-ishing abundance of wildlife. Perhaps the now-extinct Oregon condor would glide overhead.

If Lewis and Clark's Corps of Discovery retraced its route now, it would arrive in Portland after portaging around eighteen hydro-electric dams on the Columbia and Snake Rivers. They'd also encounter 250 reservoirs. Dodging oil tankers, barges, jet skis, and yachts, the explorers would see more tree farms and fish hatcheries than old growth forests and river-spanning runs of wild salmon.

My sky bridge is no time machine. It can't harvest history like new grapes from an ancient vineyard, but as I cross from one side to the other, my brain grapples with the ebb and flow of time. My wristwatch ticks, my heart beats, and I feel a temporal dislocation, a kind of time warp at odds with the clockwork of the local universe. Looking back toward the orderly, grid-patterned neigh-borhoods to the south, I see trees, roads, and houses. To the north, the face of the Columbia River floodplain reveals both the beauty marks of nature and the scar tissue of human progress. The serene green of fields and scraggily forests. The disfigurements of highways and heavy industry.

Part metaphor, part mundane reality, my sky bridge suffers from poor maintenance, yet it still delivers unexpected perks. On the narrow walkway and bike lane, clusters of blue flax, dandelions, and California poppies appear. Pigweed and teasels muscle in on the action. Like battlefield pennants, they poke up from concrete cracks, flying colors above skid marks, shattered glass, and flattened fast-food cartons. Below at a public storage facility, a pin oak grows from the concrete and creosote. Its upper branches overtop the railing, blocking my path.

In *The Log from the Sea of Cortez,* John Steinbeck says: "We have made our mark on the world, but we really have done nothing that the trees and creeping plants, ice and erosion, cannot remove in a fairly short time."

Ideally, this sky bridge should represent architectural excellence, yet it exemplifies traffic engineering at its worst. It's unsafe to walk, bicycle, or drive. The sweep of its sloppy S curve provides a world-class view, but the structure is an egregious eyesore. Before the predicted big earthquake brings it down it must be redesigned and seismically reinforced. But why throw good money after bad? Much better to partner with the forces of nature and transfigure this structure into an elevated, four-season garden like New York City's High Line Park, or South Korea's Seoullo 7017. With motorized traffic banished, a community-friendly bridge would connect green spaces, opening a bustling pollinator pathway that lures birds, bees, hikers, and bicyclists to the remaining open spaces of the floodplain.

The sound of squealing brakes jerks me back to reality. A TriMet bus slows on the curve and inches past. I wave at the driver. She smiles and waves back. She's seen me here before.

21 2020—REFUGIA IN FOUR PARTS

> **We destroyed their habitat. And now, we must rebuild it.**
>
> ARJUN ANAN, *HAMIR: THE FALLEN PRINCE OF RANTHAMBORE*

1. SMOKE AND TURTLES

On a mid-September morning, layers of sooty smoke blanketed the slough from wildfires raging through the West. Below our dock, bird tracks crisscrossed drying mud bottoms. I looked north across the water toward the four Douglas firs on the ridge. They appeared tattered, cloaked in a dirty winter fog, but we'd had no rain for months. These native conifers, long adapted to seasonal drought, drooped with thick clutches of crispy brown needles. As we unpacked the car from a road trip cut short by wildfires, our eyes stung in toxic air that exceeded 500 AQIs (air quality indicators). Inside, the house smelled like an ashtray.

"We need new furnace filters," Bruce said.

The week before, on a sticky Labor Day evening, I'd thrown open all the windows to a fiercely hot 45 mph blast and watched in fascination as the wind whipped our dining room lace curtains over the rod. Then the power went out and I began to fret about the ten gallons of summer blueberries in the freezer. The next morning, after our power returned, a fine black layer of California soot coated our tables, counters, and floors. Tiny twigs and smashed bugs plugged the window screens. I turned our AC fan on, ran the vacuum over the floors, and grabbed a box of KN95 masks, repurposing them from blocking virus to filtering smoke. Then we shut up the house and drove east along the Columbia River into an eerie orange-purple sunrise. Leaving the river, we turned north toward a log cabin near the Canadian border. For a few tranquil days, we would escape the fires—hiking, biking, and swimming with friends as if it were a normal summer.

Thus far, to quote a cable newscaster, 2020 had been a "shit show." At home during COVID's initial shutdown, unsettled weather played tricks on our spring garden. Hot, sunny May days gave way to cold, drenching rains that rotted the strawberries and drove me back to the bottom drawer for wool socks. Health experts on social media pointed to low Vitamin D levels in those with severe coronavirus reactions. Given the unpredictable weather, I fled outdoors on any day that cast shadows or topped 60 degrees.

On one of these mornings in early May, I sat on the dock in a straight-back meditation pose that promised to bring inner calm. Two years before, I had glide-pathed out of my career, but compulsive list-making and the daily need to justify my existence were still colonizing my mind. I sat struggling to follow a full breath from belly to chest and out when my eyes settled on a cottonwood log, half submerged off our dock. I'd watched this log float east and west and back again, propelled by the drainage district's relentless pumps.

Now it was stuck about ten yards off our dock. I noticed a brown bump at its fat end. Right color but wrong shape for the drab female mallard or common gadwall fluffing her feathers. Then the mound moved, and it snapped into focus. It was a turtle —the first I'd ever seen on the Buffalo Slough. Seconds later, it dove into the water.

Turtle sightings used to be more common here. Over two months in the spring of 2011, researchers from Oregon State University's Oregon Wildlife Institute scouted the Buffalo and thirty-six other slough sites, collecting data for a turtle conservation plan. The scientists traveled along the Buffalo's milelong reach in golf carts lent by Broadmoor groundskeepers. Over three surveys, they logged eighteen western painted turtles here. These are the most common of the two native Northwest species, the other being the western pond turtle. Both are considered sensitive species— priorities for conservation.

Researchers also found red-eared sliders in the slough—the species that pet stores sell as tiny hatchlings. When they grow too large for the home tank, pet owners often release the sliders, which are native to the south-central US, into the wild. If they take hold, red-eared sliders can threaten native turtles. Biologists believe this may be because the sliders nest earlier, drawing predators to the area, and gobbling up aquatic plants and insects before the native turtles can brood.

Freshwater turtles are finicky about their habitats. When the weather warms, they must leave the water to bask, exposing their carapaces, legs, and heads to UVB rays that regulate metabolism and produce the Vitamin D critical for healthy, hard shells. Half-submerged logs are ideal for basking turtles, and plentiful where cottonwoods die, rot, and topple into the slough, along with beaver-felled alders, willows, and cherry trees. Snags and branches crack and crash into the water here so frequently that the sound rarely startles us anymore.

But turtles have a hard time when trees, shrubs, or blackberry brambles crowd the banks. In spring, their nesting sites must be warmed by enough sunlight to incubate eggs. They also require pools of water deep enough for cooling dives during hot summers. In winter, they tuck into muddy sediments where they hibernate lightly (brumate), emerging only briefly when it's light and warm.

In colder climes where ponds freeze over, painted turtles can lower their body temperatures and slow their metabolism by up to 95 percent. Even so, they still require some oxygen. When ice blocks their surfacing for a lungful of air, turtles breathe through their anuses. Surrounded by blood vessels, turtle anuses absorb oxygen directly from the water in a process called cloacal respiration. Amazing, these cold weather reptiles—equipped with butt-breathing adaptations for sub-ice survival!

Oregon Wildlife Institute's report identified the Buffalo Slough as one of several promising habitats to develop a Turtle Conservation Area. With a bit of help, the placid round pool at the east end bordered by tall grasses and beached logs could house at least a hundred native turtles. But the report also included this caveat: "Replacing the restricted Buffalo Slough culvert at NE 33rd Drive . . . may help establish brood habitat and reduce sedimentation, but also may lower water levels at some times of year."

True that.

By 2020, bringing back turtles en masse to a shallower Buffalo would likely require dredging, an expensive intervention for the city's COVID-strained budget. That spring, Oregon State Parks laid off more than four hundred employees, my lovely stepdaughter, Willow (a GIS analyst) among them. Dredging is also a double-edged sword. It requires mitigating disrupted habitats and revegetating slopes. Dredged soils must also be tested for contamination and properly disposed of. Returning species to a specific location takes resources and careful follow-up, to ensure that benefits outweigh harms.

I wonder why turtles capture our attention. We buy our children tiny hatchlings, even though they don't make good pets and often die quickly with softened shells. We cry at films of turtle babies lurching across sand from cracked egg to ocean, dodging seagull beaks along their perilous path. We cross oceans to snorkel and dive with ancient sea turtles that cruise sandy bottoms.

Maybe it's their sheer survival power. Turtles appeared on earth 220 million years ago, even before snakes or crocodiles. When an asteroid offed the dinosaurs 65 million years ago, turtles were already an ancient, well-evolved species that survived the mass extinction. Nevertheless, as more wetlands, lakes, and sloughs degrade, are filled, and paved over, freshwater turtles now face steep population declines. I emailed the turtle researchers to get an update on their conservation project.

2. HOME ON THE REFUGE

In our first spring, after the cottonwoods came down, a long view opened across the Buffalo Slough to the north shore and grassy fairway rimmed with Doug firs and a black locust. To the west of the golf course, an ugly chain-link fence topped by concertina wire enclosed the power plant maintenance lot. The jarring spans of metal cried out for guerrilla landscaping. A company employee told us that the slough bank beside the power plant was city property.

One evening, Bruce wheelbarrowed two giant sequoia saplings tucked into bags of soil and mulch down our road to NE 33rd and across the bridge to the north slope of the Buffalo. I followed with shovel and rake. At dusk, we planted the saplings in front of the power plant fence, later adding a Leyland cypress, blue spruce, limber pine, and three quaking aspens. Throughout that summer's drought, I kayaked across the slough to water the saplings holding a long hose attached to our well spigot. For a Father's Day gift,

Bruce's son, Jeremy, swung an ax to clear away deadwood around the new trees. A decade later, these guerrilla plantings thrived, resisting beavers, storms, blackberry vines, and tent camps. The giant sequoias entirely obscured the fence. Success.

Closer to home, Bruce transplanted oak saplings seeded by the blue jays, coaxing them into adolescence along the borders. He sank willow and dogwood branches deep into the slough's eroding shoreline. Seemingly overnight, some of the willows grew into twenty-foot trees. On the east side of our property line, he planted evergreen shrubs—escallonia, viburnum, honeysuckle, osmanthus, ceanothus, euonymus, and Oregon grape—which soon matured into a single tall and impervious hedge. The expanding buffer formed a windbreak against fierce east winds that funneled down the Columbia Gorge.

Like the frog in a warming pot of water, I was slow to catch on to my narrowing vistas. One day, tracking two coyotes hunting rabbits near the blackberries, I had to stand on a chair to peer over the escallonia. That same winter, I failed to notice the buffleheads' migration. The curly willows and tall grasses blocked my view. The runaway vegetation had narrowed the mesmerizing swath of 300 feet of water to a tiny thumbprint of visibility.

"I can't even see the ducks anymore!" I complained.

"We're creating wildlife habitat," Bruce replied. "This was our plan all along, right?" I noted his royal "we."

But one day, without a word, he chopped down the offending escallonia, dug out the stubborn roots, mulched the soil, and planted strawberries, snapdragons, and zinnias.

"I just wanted the height down!" I was shocked but thrilled. "But now I can see the sunrise."

"Let there be light," he said.

When you look at your mate of nearly forty years and know with deep certainty you are there for the long haul, you decide to pick your battles. If I analyze our arguments over the years we've lived on the slough, they mostly come down to a chronic clash of perspectives. We find harmony in disagreement.

Bruce loves enclosure in the thick layers of shrubs and trees that bring shade, provide privacy, and attract pollinator birds and insects. I need expansive views of trees, water, and mountains. I bask in the eastern sun flooding onto our pecan floors in winter. I love following geese shadows from window to window and tracking the sunrise north to south as summer slides toward winter.

Throughout girlhood summers, I shucked corn and shelled butter beans with relatives who farmed the sandy deltas of North Carolina. In those flatlands, the horizon curves miles away. Watching a thunderstorm roll in from the coast and lying on my back to label cloud shapes were graces of childhood. Ever since, I grow cranky when trapped in cities or mountains for too many days without enough sky to scan.

With the golf course closed, we pondered the novelties of life next to a hundred acres of grasslands, wetlands, and oak savannas. The prospect of visitors, trekkers, or tent dwellers wandering up was real. With the Broadmoor winding down, a couple of strangers had already crossed the fairway onto our property. One young man in mismatched rubber boots, disoriented and agitated, crashed through the willows and into our north yard. Bruce asked him if he needed help. Moaning, the man clambered over a wood fence, breaking off several boards. Reappearing on our gravel driveway, he staggered off, shouting at a neighbor washing his car.

Bruce and the neighbor exchanged looks and shrugged. This was life in Portland, the unexpected now an everyday thing. Bruce wanted to plant more trees to block intruders. I wanted to see them coming. Our compromise was installing motion-activated lights all around.

At first, 2020's COVID pandemic shutdown silenced the roar of air traffic and industry and settled us into a comforting routine of wood fires, Dutch oven stews, and mail-order books. In those early months of pandemic, we embraced the cozy solitude, grateful to be free of Zoom meetings and work for pay. Since many of the big-box stores and recyclers stayed open, we hauled in soil, chips, gravel, and fertilizer for the garden. Without the distractions of commuting to a downtown office, air travel, and socializing, there was more time to nest at home.

In the late afternoons, we walked alleys in nearby neighborhoods where sociable chickens sported name signs and an invitation to hand feed. Along one chain-link fence, a woman had tied a row of colorful masks she'd handsewn for passersby. Down empty asphalt streets, porch dwellers waved to us like old friends. When COVID seemed like a temporary setback, the sense of shared but short-term sacrifice felt like bonds of community.

At home, Bruce pruned, weeded, and transplanted constantly, his blue wheelbarrow tooling back and forth until dusk finally drove him in, bent over with sore muscles. I made him pain-killing martinis with five olives every night, until one spring evening he announced he was going off alcohol entirely.

"To keep my immune system strong," he explained. As summer approached, we strung lights around the garden and hosted small, socially distanced patio dinners. I found solace sipping cocktails with friends.

Meanwhile, slough birds and insects seemed undaunted by 2020's vagaries. Heavy spring growth nourished dense clouds of insects, which attracted more dragonflies than ever. Swallowtail butterflies thrived. Atypical flocks of cedar waxwings raided the south garden shrubs, stripping the deep purple honeyberries before we'd even noticed they were ripe. Rows of bushtits bobbled on the outdoor light cords, waiting for their turn to bathe in the fountain. Male red-winged blackbirds swooped in to muscle the chickadees off the feeders, and whole flocks of goldfinches swarmed the thistles. A rarely seen pileated woodpecker alighted on a slough-side cedar and hammered noisily for insects.

Then the rains stopped, the heat rose, and our garden came to life. Every day I spent hours picking and freezing blueberries, drying cherry tomatoes, and blanching kale and spinach over a hot stove. One tomato plant grew so high that a friend who'd come to pick a few passed right by it, seeing instead a tree. Finally in September, wildfire smoke rolled in with the wind, the tips of the dogwoods withered, and the bats that roosted in the cottonwoods disappeared.

"I wonder if the smoke hurt their sonar," I mused to Bruce.

At last, smothered in choking air, summer 2020 ground down to a ragged end.

3. SALMON REFUGIA

The summer before COVID, Bruce and I were biking the lower slough levee when I noticed a weird formation of logs clustered against one shore. They weren't in a downstream bend where wood would ordinarily lodge or a beaver would build a dam. And the logs were cross stacked into a rectangular shape. Too neat for nature. I got off my bike to look closer.

A stack of small firs and spruces poked out of the log cross-hatch, dried needles still intact. "It's a bunch of dried Christmas trees!" I called. "Woven through that structure."

"Good for fish," said Bruce, barely glancing at it.

I climbed back on my bike, irritated by his incuriosity. As we continued west, I noted, maybe for the first time, just how bare of trees the lower slough was. The denuded levee made the logjam stick out even more.

Later, I learned what we'd seen. It was a human-engineered logjam— one of many salmon refugia built to shelter and harbor food for juvenile salmon and steelhead trout. Within these hide-outs, small fish are able to rest, feed, and grow fatter in the placid waters, protected from strong currents, predator fish, sea lions, and otters downstream.

Given the slough's torturous history, I marveled that anadro-mous fish like steelhead and salmon continue to migrate up to spawn in the lower slough's side channels, which still rise and fall with ocean tides. Tidal action no longer reaches us on the middle slough, a few miles east, where pumps and levees have severed any connection to this natural cycle. When a large carp breaches the water off our dock in the fall, I still fantasize it's a Chinook salmon come home to spawn. But of course, I know it's not.

Very little wood remains in-stream in the lower slough. When meatpacking plants, tanneries and sawmills flourished a century ago, easy access to slough water meant easy disposal of wastes, which eventually flowed into the Willamette and Columbia rivers.

New industries cleared slough shorelines of black cottonwoods, ash, and willows. But in-stream logs and root wads are vital to slow water and trap the woody debris that fish need. Wood is good for migrating fish. So, it was no surprise that as industry expanded along the lower slough slopes and overfishing persisted throughout the twentieth century, the salmon runs suffered.

To bring these fish back to the slough, the city commissioned a team of engineers, ecologists, biologists, and botanists. These experts devised an approach to build refugia like the one we saw on barges placed in-stream to reduce slope disruption. By the close of 2015, they'd anchored thirty-five engineered logjams along nine miles of the lower Columbia Slough. Each structure was a mix of conifers salvaged from tree farms, city land, and the nearby Colwood Golf Center. Packed with slash, branches, and recycled Christmas trees, the logjams left spaces large enough for small fish to hide, but small enough to host insects and block predator fish.

"We like to think of [the logjams] as buffets for the fish who eat these insects," said Melissa Brown, an environmental specialist at the Bureau of Environmental Services. "When we can pack a habitat with wood, the fish are happy."

Five years on, the logjam refugia were deemed a success. Juvenile salmon were finding food and shelter in their new engineered rest stops.

4. UPROOTED, UNHOUSED, EXCAVATED

We drove past the former Portland Meadows horse track early 2021. All the stables were down, and new Prologis buildings were up, ready for leasing to Amazon. New construction had filled the remaining wetlands there, so the clock was ticking on Prologis to offset that loss by excavating new wetlands on the now-shuttered Broadmoor Golf Course.

Meanwhile, more unhoused folks had moved nearby, seeking refuge on the roadsides. In 2020, scores of people began hunkering along a one-mile stretch of NE 33rd Drive. With a COVID no-sweep policy in effect, a host of dilapidated RVs and cars, hollowed-out boats tagged with graffiti, tents hoisted over trailers, and plywood shacks settled in.

Biking past one day, I counted sixty domiciles strung along both sides of this three-lane road, which T-boned at the Columbia River. As the weather warmed, the asphalt shoulders thronged with people tinkering under hoods, trading resources, claiming space. Against the curb, a section of iron fence enclosed a patio table, chairs, and a boat trailer piled high with scrap metal and stacks of tires.

A white wedding tent formed a breezeway between two burned-out car hulks. Tarped lean-tos stretched over the blackberries onto the Port of Portland's airport fields. Generators hummed as I biked over an orange power cord stretched across the street. Red porta potties appeared at both ends of the road, and two curbside six-foot tables overflowed with stuff for roadside denizens to give and take.

During a week of ride-byes, I heard one young couple scream at each other each day. They were half hidden behind a pastel flowered sheet tacked over their open trailer door. By week's end their trailer was gone, and another had taken its place.

With mountains of refuse rising higher each day, roadside living took on a permanent look as summer 2020 waned. I watched a man lounging on a folding chair in a sunny field while a woman gave him a haircut, a towel draped over his shoulders. Another day I squinted past two industrious bare-chested fellows blowtorching metal off a hollowed-out car. After a vehicle was scavenged and clearly uninhabitable, a green thirty-day tow label would appear.

One hot afternoon I swerved around a long ladder propped against a rusted-out RV. On top crouched a skinny young man nailing down a wooden pallet. A few days later, he was sprawled across his rooftop chaise, hands clasped behind his head, bony chest reddening in the western sun. Across the street, a buff, legless man in black muscle shirt and red bandanna knuckle-rolled his skateboard over to a man with long white hair smoking in a wheelchair. The older gent had turned his chair away from the road toward the bucolic meadow view of Mount Hood.

A quarter mile south, above Lombard Street, a single tent bloomed into another multi-shelter community. A headless mannequin stood guard, dressed in sparkly black evening gown, one arm cocked saucily on a hip. Some days her coiffed raven head rested in the grass beside a concrete Buddha. Other days, she cradled her head in her elbow. When the rains finally came, her head appeared back atop her shoulders, hair dry, face masked-up, an umbrella propped in one arm.

In this changing display, I read smoke signals of humor and resilience. Holed up on a muddy median, these tent-dwelling folks made art from found objects, seeming to give the middle finger to the pandemic, wildfire smoke, high rents, and anybody protesting their existence in public spaces.

Refugia is a term used mostly by biologists to describe areas in which life survives unfavorable conditions. By most measures, 2020 served up a host of harsh conditions. Human losses aside, biologists calculated that more than a trillion woodland animals— cougars, bear, deer, small mammals, and birds—lost their lives in the West's climate-stoked fires. These poor critters literally had nowhere to run.

But centuries of human assault have taught the wildlife a few lessons about resilience. The migrating eagles, juncos, and mergansers landed here like clockwork in October. Our birder friend Andy logged a record thirty-three species here late in the month.

The woven wood logjams made fine resting spots for juvenile salmon, and turtles flourish at Peninsula Canal and West Whitaker Pond, where the city dredged deeper pools some years ago. Turtles abound at East Whitaker Pond, too, a remarkable story of remediation told later.

But I doubt that turtle refugia will come to the Buffalo Slough anytime soon. Even I question why tight public funds should be spent dredging pools for butt-breathing brumators. Though I'd love to see more turtles off my dock, goosing nature to get them here might not make much sense.

Thousands of unhoused folks face the bone cold of a rainy Northwest winter with little more than a tent and a tarp. And the virus only widened the gulf between the "have nots" and the "have mores," the Zoom crowd and everyone else just trying to get through their day. Who is granted refuge at a time when even reality is up for grabs?

I'm putting my money on the wildlife. They've survived it all, and more.

22 THE TERRITORIAL IMPERATIVE

" I think having land and not ruining it is the most beautiful art that anybody could ever want to own.

ANDY WARHOL, *THE PHILOSOPHY OF ANDY WARHOL*

. . .

I WAS HUFFING and puffing on the steep slope of the Buffalo Slough, chopping down thorny tribes of blackberries and thistles. My routine of self-inflicted punishment felt like the labors of Sisyphus. Instead of putting shoulder to a boulder, though, I was wrestling with a hydra-like tangle of invasive plants. I hacked them to pieces, and more grew back. Seemingly overnight.

Catching my breath, I glanced up to see a very large male coyote gazing down at me. Ten yards off, the distance of an easy chip shot. Looking more wolf than coyote, he had a big head, broad shoulders, and a magnificent rusty coat. Not some scrawny back-alley scrounger, but a powerful carnivore—one who hadn't missed many meals. He sized me up, not moving, a splotchy pink and black tongue hanging from slack jaws.

I didn't move either. From behind me on the slough came a chorus of squawks. Then the thump and whoosh of flapping wings. Canada geese taking flight. The coyote gave them a glance, then trotted off, perhaps on the hunt for more suitable game.

I was encroaching on his hunting territory. At best, I was an annoying presence. Nancy and I had seen him prowling the Buffalo Slough with a pair of his hunting buddies. The Big Kahuna always ate first. This trio cruised the neighborhood, likely flushing out nutrias, muskrats, rabbits, house cats. At the shoreline they raided duck nests for eggs or hatchlings. Wads of fur, loose feathers, and purple entrails decorated the putting greens. Only a forensic expert could identify the remains.

This hunting pack left its scat everywhere, even on our back porch. Late at night, they howled and yipped as they cut through our yard. One morning, a coyote (probably a female) trotted past my office window, the bloody rag of a raccoon wagging from her jaws.

The big alpha male I encountered on the slough had most likely observed me before. I wasn't hard to miss. I wasn't just yanking weeds that day. I was trying to roust out a nest of nutrias. These destructive diggers had severely undermined the slope, creating a muddle of tunnels. Some newly planted trees had keeled over and dropped in the slough. Keeping my balance wasn't easy; I'd recently taken a tumble into the drink. Another day, I'd ensnared myself upside down in blackberry brambles, my phone, car keys, and loose change spilling out into the mud. Gravity always gets its man.

A few friends, concerned by my headlong mishaps, asked whether I had permission to work on the golf course. Clearly the slope wasn't our property.

Yes, I had permission. Well, sorta. Years before Prologis had purchased Broadmoor, I would shoot the breeze with the groundskeepers. While we dodged golf balls, they told funny stories about their daily encounters with people and wildlife.

As we talked, we tossed sticks for the Broadmoor's sweet-natured mascot, a white lab mix named Jepson. This big galoot dug for moles or splashed into the slough after mallards. He chased crows and Canada geese from the greens. At times, he also cavorted with a coyote, who would sit on his haunches at the bottom of a hill. Jepson would charge down toward his wild cousin, who at the last instant would sidestep as Jepson flew past and spun out into the mud. Barking happily, Jepson would race back up the slope and do it again. Repeat until bored.

Steve, the head groundskeeper and son of an owner, complained about the golf course's "great wall of weeds" bordering our yard.

"Our customers lose balls there all the time," he told me, "but we don't have enough staff to keep everything chopped close to your house."

I saw an opportunity to improve the good of the order. "What if I did the weeding myself? By hand."

He frowned. "That's a lot of work."

"I can do it."

"For free?"

I nodded. "I'll plant something easier to maintain. Something that's not an eyesore."

Steve shrugged and gave me a half smile.

I pointed at another maintenance-deferred spot where invasives ran eastward from our property between the golf course and slough.

"The nutrias keep digging up the bank," I said, pointing

toward the slough. "It's collapsing. I could plant stuff and haul in some deadfall. It would stabilize the slope before one of your customers goes ass-over-teakettle."

Steve thought it over for a few moments. Then nodded. No handshakes. No written agreements. A two-minute conversation had given me more work to do, but I was good to go.

Nancy was skeptical. "Your territorial imperative knows no bounds."

"Can't talk now," I said, smiling. "I'm off to plow the south forty."

In my zeal to fill any empty spaces on our own property, I'd overplanted. Transplanting surplus greenage so close to home seemed an excellent idea, for all concerned.

The next day I put on gloves, grimacing at the high jungle of uglies along our border. Making a hard right at the slough, the jungle advanced a hundred yards east to one of the Broadmoor's four pedestrian and golf cart bridges. Cottonwoods and western red cedars sagged under heavy loads of English ivy. Blackberry vines draped their limbs like victory banners. Below the tree line, nightshade, thistles, teasels, purple loosestrife, and water hemlock formed an impenetrable phalanx. Crabgrass, European frog-bit, and spiny cocklebur had claimed any uncolonized spaces.

I first removed a rusty barbed-wire fence between our properties. Seventy years old, its rotten wood posts snapped off easily, the brittle wire crumbling into dark red dust. Then I attacked the weeds. No herbicides. No weed whacker. Just machete, scythe, shovel, pruning saw, loppers, mattock, and wheelbarrow.

It was slow work. The reek of slough algae mingled with the pungency of newly mangled weeds. Pollen dust, tiny black seeds, and bedstraw stuck to my clothing. I tore out stubborn roots. Spud-shaped ones with thick gray tentacles and others that radiated laterally throughout the thin topsoil, creating dense mats. Many plants had powerful tap roots that drilled deep into the hard clay substrate, as if sucking up deep pools of petroleum.

My shovel unearthed sedimentary layers of human history. Golf balls, bottle caps, pop cans, car keys, a belt buckle, canvas loafers, a corroded sparkplug, cigarette butts. No woolly mammoth bones or decomposed humans, but one day I did discover a doll's head, a fist-sized chunk of crumbling porcelain. Sparse strands of blond hair matted its skull. Plugs of compacted dirt substituted for eyeballs. The doll had a sad round mouth. How long had it been there? What had happened to its owner? I stopped myself from thinking dark thoughts. I'd seen too many cheesy horror flicks.

I chopped and lopped the day away while golf balls whizzed past. A few beaned me, but a baseball hat and my hard head protected me. Thorns punctured my thick gloves, drawing blood. Slippery ground gave way, sending me into the slough once more.

I spoke aloud the name of every plant on death row. Pokeweed! Garlic mustard! Yellow toadflax! Tansy ragwort! None earned reprieves. Bindweed—sometimes called "wild morning glory"— was especially invasive. Its thin white roots broke off easily and resprouted quickly. In our flower garden, the bindweed's slender green vines spiraled up the stems of bachelor buttons and black-eyed Susans, forming a snug hangman's noose.

For every dozen yards liberated, I hauled in compost, sand, straw, green mulch, and wood chips. Hoping to attract more polli-nators, I back-planted coneflowers, penstemon, milkweed, and phlox. Rosemary, thyme, oregano, sage, and lavender came next. Then Oregon grape, red osier dogwood, evergold sedge, pheasant grass, willows, aspens, red alders, white oaks, and ponderosa pines.

I even put in a Pacific madrone *(Arbutus menziesii)*, a broadleaf evergreen with beautiful orange-red bark. The Salish First Nation of British Columbia revered the madrone as the tree of knowl-edge. It was never burned as firewood. According to tribal legend, a huge flood had once overwhelmed the Salish villages, but resi-dents survived by anchoring their canoes to the madrone's sturdy trunk. Given the history of massive floods in Portland, I figured it was wise to plant one.

As I worked, I reserved sunny spots for blueberries and straw-berries. Olive trees and two citrus trees—a frost-hardy Meyer lemon and mandarin orange—joined the rapidly expanding family. I scattered flower seeds. California poppies, sunflowers, zinnias, nasturtiums, snapdragons, asters, columbines, calendula, coreopsis, amaranth.

The new garden soon overspilled its original borders, creeping onto the golf course. I kept raiding my yard, but the demand for new plants was bottomless. On the lookout for good deals, I roamed the tricounty area for fresh stock. Garage sales and farmers' markets were a rich source of desirable plants. Friends offered their extras.

Many days I worked out of sight of Broadmoor's club-swinging clientele. Above me, golfers joked and swore loudly, unaware I was close by. Some walked to the top of the slope, searching for lost balls or to whiz on the knotweeds. Those who were startled by a man brandishing a machete, I assured I was no escapee from a psychiatric lock-up.

On the Buffalo's north shore, a young man with blond dreadlocks and red plaid pajama bottoms set up camp beneath three cottonwoods bordering the course. During daylight hours, he cloistered inside a red tent, but at sunset he paced back and forth near the power plant, screaming and sobbing about a woman who'd apparently wronged him. His cries carried across the water. Other neighbors heard him as well. One complained that the man's loud keening gave her teenage daughter nightmares. Worried that he needed professional intervention, I walked over to alert the utility company.

"Corporate is on it," a front desk employee said.

A few weeks later, workers arrived and cut down the cottonwoods. Inspecting the jumble of downfall, I found only a crushed suitcase, a pair of boxer shorts, and a pizza box. No red tent.

Afterward, workers sprayed the shoreline there, working east to west. Making a few phone calls, I learned that the City of Portland had contracted with an outfit to remove noxious weeds. They were using Rodeo, a broad-spectrum glyphosate-based herbicide manufactured by Dow AgroSciences. Alarmed, I contacted local and state agencies. A city employee told me they routinely sprayed herbicides to control the slough's invasive plants.

"Nobody likes doing it," she told me, "but it's cheap and fast."

Without notice, a biologist from the Oregon Department of Agriculture showed up at our house one week later.

"I'm here about the spraying you reported," he told me.

I invited him down to our dock and pointed to the opposite shoreline, indicating where the spraying had left a wide swath of dried brown plants.

"I've read the research," I told him. "Glyphosates are toxic for fish, birds, and plants. People, too."

Raising his eyebrows, he reached into his satchel and pulled out an agency manual the size of a telephone book. Opening it, he fanned through the pages, stopping at one with flyspeck print.

"The EPA classifies glyphosates as environmentally safe," he said, "You must be talking about European research—not American research."

I chose not to argue. Dow always got the last word. Like other agrochemical corporations, it determined US public policy on the use of toxic chemicals. Its executives routinely bounced between government service and lobbying, ensuring that environmental laws didn't curb the use of controversial pesticides and herbicides. When criticized, they claimed they were helping to "feed the world."

In the meantime, my battle continued against invasives on our side of the slough. Blackberries and thistles counterattacked, reclaiming contested turf. Flexing their limbs, they rammed thorny snouts through three feet of hard-packed wood chips, and like Russian weightlifters on steroids, tossed aside large logs.

The nutrias dug burrows, forming air pockets beneath the roots of plants, shrubs, and trees. Emerging from their underground lairs late at night, they gnawed down willows, aspens, and alders. Each day fresh mole mounds created hell's little half acre of overturned earth. I complained to Nancy, but she wasn't sympathetic.

"You're working yourself to death on somebody else's property."

"If nature doesn't care about property lines," I mumbled, "why should I?"

As I swung my mattock next to the slough, kayakers paddled past, ogling the wildlife.

A Columbia Slough Watershed Council volunteer pointed out a western tanager perched on a nearby cottonwood snag, its orange-red head, black wings, and yellow plumage aglow in the summer twilight.

"Most birds get that red color from plant pigments," she explained, "but tanagers get theirs from eating wasps, beetles, caterpillars, and ants."

I learned the plant pigment was rhodoxanthin, a substance found also in yew and honeysuckle.

On weekends, a shirtless man with shaggy gray hair sprawled himself flat across his kayak and used a specialized pole and net to pluck golf balls from the muck. One day, a group of elementary-age kids drifted into view on inner tubes, no supervising adults in sight. They hooted and screeched as they shot water cannons at each other. An incongruous sight, like seeing icebergs in the Sahara, but the slough specialized in incongruity.

Shortly thereafter, a windstorm toppled a large hemlock at a neighbor's house. He chain sawed it into portable sizes and told me I could have whatever I could haul off. I loaded up the first hemlock round into my blue wheelbarrow and trundled my prize down the street. I planned to use these rounds to bolster the slough's eroding slope, and to create protected spots for my new plantings. As I walked toward the Broadmoor, a car sped past me. Then it stopped and backed up. It was my brother-in-law, Jack.

"I thought you were a homeless person. Then I recognized the blue wheelbarrow."

So it went. Through spring downpours, summer heat waves, and winter blasts, I slowly revegetated the weed-choked wilderness. Successes often dissolved into failures, the rough tumbledown of seasons taking its periodic toll. But I kept at it over the next year, donating the requisite quart of blood and pound of flesh to a project I wholeheartedly believed in.

I wore work wounds like combat medals. Scratches, gashes, skin rashes, swollen joints, pulled muscles, sprained ankles, split fingernails, allergy-inflamed eyes, but no broken bones. After my right elbow swelled painfully, my doctor blamed it on water hemlock *(Cicuta douglasii)*. This invasive plant contains cicutoxin, a poison that can cause frothing, convulsions, and comas.

Then a scratch from a blackberry thorn became infected. I

developed a high fever. My hands shook uncontrollably. My left leg turned red and swelled to three times its normal size. I had cellulitis—then sepsis. I spent five days in the hospital hooked up to a variety of machines and monitors as an IV tube dribbled antibiotics into my veins. Each morning, I received an injection in my stomach. A precaution against blood clots. As I slept, the medications messed with my mind. I hallucinated myself as a spirit set adrift in a nebulous nether realm. I struggled to take back possession of my body, to regain entrance to the animal comforts of my known world. I told my doctor about it.

"It's kinda dispiriting," I explained, attempting a weak joke.

"A hospital stay can be very dispiriting," he said, straight-faced. "Bad dreams are typical."

Nancy remained at my bedside all day. Capitalizing on my weakened state, she demanded I hire a gardener. "You can't keep expanding," she said. "It's gotten to be too much for you."

I stared at my hospital dinner plate. Chicken cubes, mashed potatoes, gravy, and an iceberg lettuce salad with a dollop of ranch dressing. I read the ingredients on the carton of vanilla-flavored ice cream. "Contains bioengineered products."

We discussed the difficulty of finding somebody who understood our bewildering mosaic of microhabitats. I wasn't even sure I understood our yard enough to coach a stranger.

"Gardeners don't come cheap," I said.

"Doesn't matter," she replied. "Your health comes first. Don't try to weasel out of this. "Promise me you'll hire some help."

"I promise." I sounded like a sulking child.

Recuperating at home, I spent weeks trying to hire a gardener. Portland apparently had a shortage of people willing to do this kind of physical work. It was a seller's market. People who returned my calls wanted at least $50 an hour for wielding a pair of loppers. One told me he didn't climb stepladders.

"Heights kinda weird me out," he explained. "I like to keep my feet planted on the ground."

Six friends arrived one weekend to help prune and weed our property. Hard at work the entire morning, they accomplished the impossible. But relying on friends wasn't sustainable.

"You're still on the hook for what you promised," Nancy reminded me.

Reassuring her I wouldn't give up, I put on a compression sock and returned to brute labor on the golf course. In my absence, no miraculous improvements had occurred. In fact, the invasives had returned with a vengeance. While the gardener's away, the weeds will play. So will the nutrias. They had taken out the small aspens, red alders, and willows. They had even hauled off several three-foot oaks.

I bent my back to the task again, working to regain lost ground, more aware that thorns, stickers, and sharp branches harbored billions and billions of bacteria, every one eager to break through my skin and mob my veins and arteries. Even on hot days, I wore protective clothing and gear. After each day's work, Nancy conducted a body check for scratches, welts, and puncture wounds.

It was slow, stop-and-start grunt work, but my stoop labor eventually yielded results. I got the temporary upper hand on a rogue's gallery of creepers, sneakers, and berserkers. My plant-it-and-they-will come strategy seemed to be working. With every millimeter of progress came a surge in animal activity. Stopping work near dusk, I watched flights of iridescent tree swallows. Performing their aerial dances in the fading light, they swooped through clouds of gnats, harvesting small magpie moths. I saw bats, too. Not many, but enough to lift my spirits.

On warm days, I dropped my loppers and watched Anna's and rufous hummingbirds sipping from penstemon blossoms. More pollinators appeared. Honeybees and bumblebees. Carpenter and mason bees. Elfin brown butterflies and swallowtails. Thread-waisted wasps and bald-faced hornets. Even "mess and soil" polli-nators—such as orange-headed soldier beetles—fed, mated, and pooped on recently planted goldenrod or spirea.

Sparrows and spotted towhees worked the underbrush, snap-ping up spiders, aphids, and leafhoppers. Downy woodpeckers and northern flickers drilled into the deadfall. The occasional sharp-shinned hawk, with the maneuverability of an X-wing starfighter, pursued nuthatches and sparrows through a Death Star mazework of salmonberry branches.

Turning over logs, I discovered garter snakes, a favorite food of herons, hawks, raccoons, and crows. I picked up one of these stripey little guys, and as it wriggled in my hands, a foul-smelling yellow substance slimed my fingers. Snake poop. An effective defense strategy.

Pleased with what I was doing, Steve gave permission to edge further out into the golf course. I dug up giant clods of dandelion-colonized grass, chopped them up for mulch, and plopped down a fresh batch of beneficial plants. I broadcast seeds everywhere. In time, the Broadmoor's golfers ogled the throngs of colorful wild-flowers, the profusion of strawberries and blueberries. Bees, butter-flies, and birds swirled close to the greens. Some golfers stopped to talk about their own gardens. We swapped advice about plants and pests. I made sure to give the groundskeepers credit for everything, downplaying my own heavy-handed role.

Then . . .in the fall of 2020, my cozy off-the-record relation-ship with Broadmoor ended. Prologis had purchased the property. No more golfers. No more handshake arrangement with the groundskeepers.

When John van Staveren, the senior scientist overseeing the future wetlands development, came for a meeting with Nancy, I told him what I'd been up to.

"This isn't my land, but I enjoy taking care of it," I said.

John smiled. "Be pretty hard to move all these plants, wouldn't it?"

He walked our property line, noting the survey markers poking up from the thick firethorn, fountain grass, and sawbeak sedge I'd planted. He spoke the name of every plant, scrutinizing my work down to the bridge. His face remained expressionless.

"Leave everything here for now," he said, returning. He pointed to a large Santa Barbara Mexican bush sage (*Salvia leucantha.*) "The non-natives will probably have to go. The City of Portland doesn't want them next to the slough."

"How long do I have before the hammer comes down?"

He laughed. "About a year. More or less. We'll have to see."

23 HEAVY METAL—A SLOUGH REMEDIATION STORY

❝ **Progress is measured at the speed at which we destroy the conditions that sustain life.**

GEORGE MONBIOT, "UK GUARDIAN"

. . .

A GLINT of ocher in the roadside grass caught my eye. Walking the neighborhood at sunset on the second pandemic spring, I bent to the curb to find a shiny coil of copper cable, about three feet in diameter. No businesses or houses were close by. Still, I looked left, right, and behind me before picking up the coil and quickly moving on.

Beside me, Bruce laughed. "Don't worry. Nobody's around to jump you for it."

I didn't know a lot about copper, but I knew it held value. A few days later, I took the heavy coil to a metal recycling business nearby, Metro Metals Northwest. They gave me $30 for it. Thirty bucks, no questions asked. This fed my suspicion that the copper coil had probably been lifted from a nearby worksite and dropped by the thief, perhaps spooked by a passerby.

Scrap metal recycling, I learned, is a lucrative business. People and businesses sell all manner of scrap. They bring in construction beams, metal plates, pipes, tubes, wiring, old automobiles, boat and railroad materials, radiators, aluminum siding, cans and lids, batteries and electronics, brass locks—even tarnished silver flatware and jewelry. Lead and aluminum are the most common nonferrous scrapped metals.

Other more valuable metals, both precious and toxic, are retrieved from scrap, like the copper cable I sold. Silver sluiced from X-rays and photo film, zinc pried from batteries and pipes, gold from electronics, and nickel extracted from stainless steel.

After 2020, as platinum values skyrocketed, local thieves kicked into high gear, stealing catalytic converters out of cars seemingly block by block. These thefts became so common in Oregon that the legislature passed a bill, effective January 2022, that required metal recycling companies to purchase converters only from commercial sellers, with the car's VIN (vehicle identification number) and license number retained.

Recently, I'd had a gold dental crown replaced. Glued in by a college boyfriend in dental school, the crown had survived nearly a half century of popcorn, pistachios, and ice-crunching before finally developing a hole in the middle. Prying it out took my dentist several minutes and lots of grinding. After it dislodged and

I could swallow, I asked, "Do you get anything for melting these down?"

"For sure," he said. "Gold is high now. We don't even do full caps like this anymore. We just fill in the drilled parts with gold."

So I asked for my gnarled little chunk of gold for "sentimental reasons" and the bemused hygienist handed it over, zipped into a tiny plastic bag. Maybe I'll look up the boyfriend, email a pic of it with my thanks, then sell it at one of those Bring Us Your Gold places.

The recycling services I researched also advertised high returns for silver. I found myself making a quick calculation of what I might get for my mother's silver flatware, serving bowls, and gravy urn. Coveted wedding gifts for her 1940s marriage. But who uses a gravy boat anymore or polishes silver for dinner guests? Stuffed into an old duffel bag, these artifacts slowly blacken and gather dust in our attic. I have little desire to bring them down to clean up and use. But I think I'll leave the bag up there, at least for now. Those who follow can decide what to do with it. Most likely they'll haul it all down to melt.

It's amazing the toil that's required to extract the good stuff from metal scrap. Recycling companies grind, blast, roast, and melt the materials they buy. They use gas, metal, and plasma torches to cut metal away from wood and plastic. To isolate and purify precious metals, a host of chemical processes are applied—chlorination, plating, leaching, chemical separation, dissolution, reduction, and galvanizing.

For better handling, scrap materials are shredded, baled, and compacted. Unavoidably, these activities create smoke, dust, fumes, and effluents that contain metal particles which can settle on soil and wash into stormwater.

Since 1994, Metro Metals has run its scrap recycling business on a five-acre lot on Columbia Blvd. Just downslope from the company, and less than two miles east of us, lies East Whitaker Pond, a shallow section of the twenty-five-acre Whitaker Ponds Nature Park. East Pond connects to the deeper West Whitaker Pond, which features a half-mile nature trail, an eco-roof gazebo, and a canoe launch into Whitaker Slough. Like the Buffalo,

Whitaker Slough discharges into the main stem of the Columbia Slough. On the map, Buffalo and Whitaker Sloughs resemble twins, both of their narrow necks looping north like an esophagus.

For its first fourteen years, Metro Metals' untreated stormwater flowed directly into East Whitaker Pond. Like other businesses with slough outfalls, it was eventually required to meet tighter environmental regulations. In 2008 the company installed a state-of-the-art stormwater treatment system. But soil and sediments hold onto contaminants over time. Even after Metro Metals upgraded its system in 2013, East Whitaker Pond harbored a witches' wish list of toxins.

When Portland acquired Whitaker Ponds in 1998, Metro, the Columbia Slough Watershed Council, and scores of volunteers partnered with city bureaus to transform the area. After removing over two thousand tires, they planted black cottonwood trees and thousands of other native plants where denuded lots once housed heavy equipment dealers and a junkyard. Now in the summer, hummingbirds, butterflies, and bees flit among wildflowers and native shrubs, pollinating as they go. Migratory birds stop by.

The Whitaker Ponds Nature Park is a jewel in the crown of the middle slough, a home for woodpeckers, rabbits, beavers, garter snakes, osprey, dragonflies, otters, and wood ducks. It's a cooling oasis for wildlife tucked among small businesses that peddle pallets, recycle yard waste, and sell auto parts.

One late fall day, I walked West Whitaker's nature trail, enjoying the crunch of dry leaves underfoot. I came up to a birder who shared a phone shot she'd taken of a barred owl perched in a bare cottonwood. More active than other owls during the day, the barred owl has a round brownish head, which faced the photographer with a full-on gaze: "What's up with YOU?" it seemed to demand. Birders have spotted and logged nearly 170 species in the nature park. Water, trees, and native shrubs—along with a "no dogs allowed" rule—are a come-hither lure for wildlife to stop or stay on Whitaker Ponds.

I've never walked around East Whitaker Pond. Its six acres are a protected wildlife area, with no public access, paddling, or fishing permitted. Like Buffalo Slough, East Pond is often very shallow during low water, and only three to six feet deep in high water. It recharges solely from ground and stormwater. Despite its seasonal dryness, East Whitaker Pond is home to a declining population of western painted turtles, as well as many small mammals, beavers, and birds.

Under the direction of the Department of Environmental Quality (DEQ), Metro Metals agreed to conduct soil, sediment, and stormwater investigations in 2012–13. Scientists found contaminants of concern at nine locations in East Pond's sediments. PCBs, cadmium, copper, and lead tested above bioaccumulation screening levels.

Not surprisingly, these nasties clustered below Metro Metals' outfall, almost certainly from the company's legacy stormwater runoff. Hot spots of contaminants also showed up in six upland soil samples, including zinc, copper, chromium, lead, and mercury.

Valuable metals can sicken people and animals. Cadmium and lead from recycled batteries and paints; copper and zinc from cables and car alloys; chromium and mercury used in paints, dyes, and stainless steel. All these metals are toxic when inhaled as fumes, absorbed through the skin, or digested in food. The Occupational Safety and Health Administration (OSHA) requires metal recycling companies to protect workers from contact exposure. Ironically, one of these methods, hosing down machinery to settle dust, can flush contaminants directly into soil or stormwater.

In 2016, Metro Metals was directed to pay for cleanup and remediation of East Whitaker Pond, including the pond's sediments and upland soils. The goal was to prevent birds, mammals, fish, and benthic organisms (plants and animals that live on water bottoms) from direct exposure to PCBs and toxic metals.

A full-on remediation project may seem shockingly complex to a layperson. It did to me. It began with clearing out all existing vegetation. Then city ecologists found and relocated the live turtles in the pond, prior to draining it.

Next, heavy machinery moved in on newly constructed roads to dredge and remove the most contaminated sediments for disposal offsite (over 1,800 cubic yards, about 150 truckloads). Contractors then sprayed activated carbon over the moderately

contaminated areas and laid a cap of clean sand on less contaminated areas. After that, they returned large pieces of cleaned-up
wood to the shoreline, anchored basking logs, and laid back banks
to ease access for turtle nesting. Finally, they revegetated the
uplands with a diverse array of native plants.

Activated carbon is the primary remedy for treating contaminated sediments in situ. This is the same material doctors pump
into people's stomachs when they overdose or ingest poisons.
Carbon molecules contained in charcoal are processed into small,
low-volume pores. These tiny particles present lots of surface area
for chemical adsorption.

Sprays of activated carbon particles adhere to PCBs and other
contaminants in the sediments. They lower the toxins' mobility
(their release from sediments into water) and their bioavailability
(their uptake into plants and animals). Put simply, the carbon binds
to the bad stuff, and keeps it where it lies.

The project at East Whitaker Pond took place between May
and October 2021. Contaminated sediments were trucked to a
landfill licensed to contain them safely. Long-term monitoring of
water, soil, and sediments will help certify that toxins remain below
bioaccumulation levels.

Sarah Miller, a natural resources project manager at DEQ, has
overseen clean-up projects along the slough for over a decade.
"Honestly, this one went really well," she told us. "Metro Metals
was a good steward . . . responsive, taking comments and making
the changes needed for a successful project."

When the pond was drained at the outset, only eight turtles
were found and relocated west. Two weeks after the project was
completed, East Whitaker Pond had refilled naturally from autumn
rains and groundwater. Shortly thereafter, a happy surprise greeted
observers. Dozens of turtles appeared on the newly anchored, half-
submerged logs!

Laura Guderyahn, turtle expert and natural areas ecologist for
Portland Parks and Recreation, has a theory about this good
fortune. "We took all these protections for the turtles, but we found
we didn't need them. Enough water remained in East Pond to keep

the mud in liquid form, so the turtles seemed perfectly happy hiding in the mud by day and coming up to feed at night."

East Whitaker Pond offers a textbook case of successful slough cleanup. The responsible party was identified and engaged. The clean-up project was executed on time with tangible outcomes.

After the phone call with Laura, I was captivated by the image of dozens of turtles, so shy by nature, burrowed deeply into pond mud, waiting out the thundering noise and vibration of heavy dredging machines before emerging into long late summer evenings to feed. Then I remembered that resilience was baked into their carapaces. These reptiles survived the comet that wiped out the dinosaurs sixty-five million years ago. As climate change accelerates to remake the known world, the turtles may get a last word.

24 REWILDING

❝ **Let us put our minds together and see what life we can make for our children.**

CHIEF SITTING BULL, PLEA TO US GOVERNMENT REPRESENTATIVES

NOVEMBER 2022

Two weeks before Thanksgiving, we sit at the kitchen banquette discussing this book, three years in the writing, and almost finished. It's a blustery fall day. Time to stay indoors, wear a sweater, drink tea. The conversation drifts toward two friends, both grappling with dementia. We recall dinner parties with them. Hikes in the Columbia Gorge and along the Elrod Canal. The more we talk, the sadder we get. Tears follow. The sudden loss of mind or body can make an argument for a hostile universe. Still as the Buddha said, we've all accepted the "terms of existence." And today existence feels sweet and precious.

Walking the garden, we scare a feral cat off a dead spotted towhee *(Pipilo maculatus)*. The towhee is a ground forager, and when it searches for seeds and small bugs, it has a two-footed backward "double-scratching" hop that distinguishes it from other sparrows. Easy for a cat to ambush.

After burying the bird, we decide to take a walk on the former golf course to shake off our anger about the towhee kill. A cold east wind blows steadily down the Columbia Gorge, so we zip into winter coats. Dried leaves, a plastic sack, and broken branches blow past, snagging on the desiccated stalks of thistles and teasels.

Even in this wind, birds forage along the margins of the slough. Sparrows, house finches, black-capped chickadees, and flickers scout the deadfall and underbrush for seeds, nuts, worms, grubs, and beetles. Blue jays and starlings face off in a red cedar, squabbling over a block of suet we've anchored there. Across the Buffalo Slough, two snowy egrets wade in the shallows, fishing. Gus usually drives them off, but not today. Our heron is sleeping on the job.

Truck sirens wail along Columbia Blvd, perhaps headed toward a wind-stoked fire. On cue, coyotes howl in response. Sirens always set them off. Coyote songs mingle with the siren songs of civilization. They sound close by, but we can't see them. Thickets of goldenrod have sprouted high on all eighteen greens, obscuring our view. Do the coyotes think they're communicating with another pack? Or does instinct trigger these yips? Impossible to know.

Close to our property, we inspect two tall cottonwoods. A beaver has chewed halfway through both. The Buffalo Slough is unusually high, and rising water lifts all beavers. This one capitalized on the opportunity to sharpen its teeth. The cottonwoods are goners. In a strong wind, this pair of leafy galoots could crack, snap, and topple onto our house. So, we've notified Prologis, and an arborist will head over to assess the threat.

Around our house, raccoons will soon hibernate in the rotting cottonwoods. There are a lot left to choose from. On warm days, they loaf on the trees' mid-level limbs, snoozing the day away, their legs and tails hanging loose. Through our years living here, we've witnessed generations of raccoons. They march out of their tree condos, as if on parade, toddle through our yard triggering the motion lights, and stop on our neighbor's porch to help themselves to a bowl of cat food. Sometimes the adults lose parts of their tails from fights with other raccoons, or close calls with predators. Young and old die fast, many along the highways.

Last June, two of our neighbor's dogs killed a mother raccoon at the base of a Babylon weeping willow. Afterward, her three kits emerged and wandered the slough shoreline, crying. They were hungry. Then they went silent. A few days later, we caught the strong smell of death coming from a clump of yellow flag irises bordering the slough. Fearing what we'd find, we searched the shoreline for the source of the stench but found nothing. No baby raccoon bodies or telltale wads of fur.

Just west of the beaver-chewed trees, we discover that nutrias have struck again, taking out a long line of curly willows and euonymus (spindle tree) we'd replanted in the spring. Also a few white oak, and red alder saplings. Only the stumps are left, the bark stripped off.

Directly south looms a fifty-foot wall, which obscures the late fall sunrise. Stretching almost a half mile east to west, the wall is made from hundreds of earth-packed wire baskets, two feet high, row after row stacked atop each other. Next spring, the dump trucks will return to raise the wall another twenty feet. In technical jargon, it's a "Mechanically Stabilized Earth retaining wall," or MSE. Gravity stabilizes the massive structure, enabling it to hold enough cubic yards of backfill to bury a football field. At fifty feet, the wall is already high enough to overshadow our property. We call it the White Walker Wall, for the massive one built in *Game of Thrones* to block the armies of the living dead. Soon a new warehouse/distribution center will perch atop it, and a nature park will spread over the hundred-plus acres below.

We continue northeast toward the airport, stopping to scrape globs of wet clay from our shoes. Leaping over a ditch, we cross two portable steel bridges spanning the Buffalo and main sloughs, then stumble through an upchuck of gravel, rocks, and dead trees. More than ever, walking here is an ankle-twisting ordeal. We step in mole holes, and trip over deadfall and brambles. Sand traps, fairways, paths, and roads have vanished into a tangle of weeds. Bulldozers have scraped other debris into muddled heaps of asphalt, rusty irrigation pipes, golf balls, and grass clods. It looks like an archaeological midden, holding a bygone century of humanity's pastimes.

After moving to the neighborhood in 2008, we walked this land whenever we could, exploring waterways, forests, and open spaces. Bragging to friends about our knowledge of the terrain, we joked that we could sleepwalk our way around the golf course. Since Prologis began bioengineering, we get lost easily. It's a terra incognita scraped clean of reliable landmarks. Hundreds of trees are gone. Enormous mounds of rock and dirt make us feel like we've blundered into the Land of the Giant Gophers.

Where vegetation remains, it's still slow going through thick growths of thistles, teasels, and waist-high grass, much of it flattened and matted with copious deer, rabbit, and coyote scat. A few patches of hardy tall grasses are a lovely tawny color, and soft under foot. In these spots, it's easy to imagine lions approaching across the veldt.

Stopping next to a jumble of toppled trees, we inspect the trunk of an Oregon ash. In old Norse mythology, Yggdrasill was a giant ash that supported the entire universe. This ash shows the telltale marks of the Emerald ash borer *(Agrilus planipennus)*, a destructive beetle from northeastern Asia. Its larvae have scored the wood beneath the bark with a complex network of S-shaped galleries. Boring deep into the ash's cambium, adult beetles eat out the hearts of ash trees.

Further on, we find the remains of a large raptor, its feathers and bones scattered across a rust-colored mat of pine needles. It's such a mess we can't identify the species. Something has eaten it. Probably a coyote, but how did it catch it? Perhaps the crows drove the raptor to ground where a coyote pounced on it, making use of the new high grass cover.

This property, now called Prologis Broadmoor Park, no longer looks like a golf course. A mazework of bright orange plastic silt fencing crisscrosses the muddy ground. From a distance it resembles landscape art, a Christo and Jeanne-Claude exhibition in dayglo orange showcasing slaughtered trees. Giant sequoias, cedars, ponderosas, Douglas firs, incense-cedars, birches, willows, locusts. Brush rabbits and ground-foraging birds shelter in the jumbled assemblage of shattered trunks and fractured limbs.

Despite the look of things now, this property will undoubtedly become more wildlife-friendly than the golf course ever was. Maintaining a fussy monoculture of grass, sand traps, shrubbery, and trees requires money, effort, and toxic chemicals. Oceans of pesticides, herbicides, and synthetic fertilizers. All this gunk drains into the watershed and into the bloodstreams of animals. Watering a golf course is expensive, even in the rain-soaked Pacific Northwest. The Broadmoor pumped most of its irrigation water directly from the slough. Choosing between a golf course and a bioengineered wetland is a no brainer. Mother Nature agrees.

But wild animals and native plants don't operate on an industrial scale. Viable habitats can't be cloned, brewed in a chemical vat, or printed on a 3D computer. If we smash up a car, it's sometimes repairable. When we smash up the natural world, returning it to working order is like trying to reverse the arrow of time.

At the far northeastern corner of the Broadmoor, we see five freshly felled giant sequoias. Only one remains at that spot, standing guard to the airport's south runway. To the west, a broad trench forms a moat around two dozen remaining giant sequoias.

A twenty-foot pile of their recently bulldozed brethren rises from the mud. A postmodern ziggurat? A pickup sticks game for giant beaver gods? No. The sequoias have been bulldozed together to make wetlands refugia, affordable homes for unhoused critters. Everything we view is part of a wildlife sanctuary in the making.

Arriving finally at the northwest end of the Broadmoor, we clearly see now where all the dirt came from that packs the towering wall next to our house. Several gargantuan holes, acres long, have been gouged out from the earth. Now water fills them two–three feet deep. These vast declivities look more like lakes than wetlands. Ducks and geese have already arrived. The sound of them is deafening, the sight of them a flight of imagination. As we stand gaping at it all, this sweeping spectacle evokes images of Pleistocene hunters and gatherers stalking waterfowl, tossing stone-weighted fishing nets, and harvesting bulrushes, reeds, and wapato.

From the middle of one lake, a rubbery coyote decoy pokes its black nose above water. It doesn't fool these Canada geese, which are a huge headache near airports. No pilot wants to attempt an emergency landing in the Columbia River, their jet brought down by goose strike.

Gazing across this serendipitous expanse of water, we dub it Lake Broadmoor, awed by the complex feat of environmental engineering. The dead trees haven't gone to waste. Wetlands bioengineers have shoveled and sculpted jumbled masses of logs and limbs throughout, providing habitat and roots for raptors, waterfowl, and other animals. Resembling works of modern art, several tree trunks rise improbably from the water. Dead ponderosa and giant sequoias are now vertical towers, anchored upside down in the water, snaky roots reaching for the sky. Tangles of wood transformed into nests for ospreys.

For the first time, we can see the big picture. It's now possible to envision how Broadmoor Nature Park might just become the crown jewel of the nineteen-mile Columbia Slough, setting the standard for the development of future green spaces. With enough money, machinery, and imagination, nature has a chance to rebound.

These build-it-and-they-will-come wetlands will invite flickers to hunt and peck among the white oaks. Stoats to snag rabbits, herons to spear bullfrogs. Beavers to chomp cottonwoods, ospreys to snatch carp, kingfishers to dive for red swamp crawdads. It's all possible.

We decide to trace the rugged lake perimeter, which horseshoes around a spit of forested land. Spring-planted water plantains and sedges form a bright expanse of apple green, rimmed by willows and cattails. Bare root alders, white oaks, and grand firs surround the slopes. Many tiny trees failed to take root in the hard clay soil, but the survivors seem determined, and Prologis's landscaping contractor will return next spring to replant.

We know the water here is temporary. This isn't supposed to be a lake—it's one of the new seasonal wetlands. In the future, if too much water accumulates, it must be quickly drained off before the waterfowl claim it as home.

As we follow the shoreline, a few killdeers hop and fly ahead of us, searching for snails and spiders. They are newcomers here. These elegant plovers have two black breast bands that accentuate their rich assemblage of brown, white, and rufous-colored feathers. A friend who volunteers for Audubon told us that crows and raccoons prey on killdeers, but these birds are very cagey. If a predator threatens their nests, they pull a "broken wing act," flying a short distance, stopping, then flying again. This nifty trick draws off the would-be predator, and when the killdeer senses the danger has passed, it flies back to its nest, mission accomplished.

Animal tracks score the mud. Mostly birds, deer, raccoons, and coyotes. No nutrias, muskrats, or beavers yet. These critters have yet to discover the new all-you-can-eat hotspot on the slough. But news travels fast here. Soon the hefty herbivores will arrive in force to crunch on cattails, willows, and trees.

It takes us an hour to walk a slip'n'slide circle around the lake-cum-wetland, trees bowing in the wind, the sky milky blue. We stop often, taking in the sights and marveling how water isn't just the universal solvent. It's also the universal magnet, attracting a wealth of wildlife.

The wind riffles the water. Everything shimmers and blurs, as if one big pitcher of sunlight is spilling a full load of photons onto the world. Land. Plants. Animals. Thirsty for light, they gulp it down. We're also thirsty. Winter is coming. We wish we could cup our hands and capture this golden November sunlight and hold it close like a firefly from a summer evening.

Stopping to sit beneath a lone giant sequoia, we imagine how this area looked when Lewis and Clark paddled past here. They had no idea these wetlands rested on a hard pillow of Columbia River basalts, or that prehistoric predators once prowled the marshes. In 1805, this real estate was still hydrologically connected to a riparian network of springs, streams, and rivers. It was drop-down-dead beautiful. In their journals, Lewis and Clark described the diversity in this watershed, extolling "thickly timbered land-scape" and "fowls flying in every direction." A mere hundred years later, the source of that diversity was drained, filled, channeled, and then defiled.

John Muir once complained that he was "degenerating into a machine for making money." After the Corps of Discovery paved the path for Euro-American pioneers, the slough and its wetlands degenerated into a money-making machine. But in the latter half of the twentieth century, people with great foresight stepped up to stop the destruction and heal the slough's deep wounds. Mourning what was lost, they committed to protect what was left.

From our close-in view, the slough remains a hybrid habitat, an ever-shifting battleground of conflicting values and interests. Many good people with expertise toil continuously to make things better, working to bring back turtles, freshen water, monitor outfalls, and cap sediments. Still the slough can use more helping hands. A new generation of homegrown John Muirs, Rachel Carsons, and Aldo Leopolds to cradle and nurture this "thin ribbon of connectivity."

The gravitas of the giant sequoia invites a contemplative mood. As we look out over the water, we discuss how to reweave whole cloth from this ecosystem's fragile threads. It's not just a matter of money, time, and effort. It's a matter of consciousness and compassion. What kind of caring and mindful relationship should we have with plants and wildlife? With water, air, and land? For us, respecting our planet as a living, conscious being is the crux of being human.

Muir also wrote that "the clearest way into the Universe is through a forest wilderness." Forests, deserts, grasslands, rivers, canyonlands, wetlands—even the Columbia Slough. They all offer portals to the universe. But we can only walk through them holding the natural world close to our hearts.

Approaching two decades here, we still find ourselves both awed and baffled by the beauty-and-the-beast character of the 32,000-acre Columbia Slough watershed. It's a corridor of countless contradictions. Sometimes it's the Slough of Despond. Sometimes a stricken water snake caught out in hostile territory. More often, the slough provides a Magical Mystery Tour of a water world neighborhood. One that reveals the resplendence and resiliency of nature.

It's late afternoon, and autumn dusk comes early to this latitude. Reluctantly, we stand, brushing needles from our jeans. It will take close to an hour to walk home. Rounding the path to our property, we nearly trip over two fat adult raccoons ambling away, completing their route from the neighbor's cat bowl and through our garden to their cubbyhole at the base of a western red cedar.

Maybe those are the kits from the summer, one of us said to the other. Maybe they made it after all.

END

ACKNOWLEDGMENTS

In recent years, Portland lawns have disappeared, urban gardening has taken off, and year-round kale and collards are a common sight in every neighborhood. Unlike many parts of our country, our city is fortunate to have abundant, clean drinking water, gravity-fed from Mount Hood's foothills and back-stopped by three nearby aquifers. Clean water is a resource we cannot take for granted. We are fortunate to live in a city that cares about protecting its waters.

We would never have found and made our "vest-pocket Valhalla" in Portland without the support and guidance of many good people and organizations. First, Mark Barham, our friend and realtor who stuck with us through nearly two years of property searches, convincing us finally to take a look at the little house on the slough. Our architect and designer, Keyan Mizani of eMZed Architecture, created the vision for reconfiguring interior spaces and adding glass to open our home to nature. It never ceases to awe.

It's a tall task to remodel an eighty year old home and retain its pine-cabin hominess, but our general contractors Dale Jones and Jeffrey Krater worked magic throughout, blending old and new wood artfully, modernizing tight spaces and creatively problem solving engineering challenges, while honoring the character of the log home that Mr. Giese built. Our friend Dude Edwards accepted the daunting challenge of working in slough sediments to build a new dock. He and his lovely wife, longtime friend and colleague Nicky Martin Edwards recently found their own Valhalla – twenty-eight acres of actual countryside to farm! We also thank another engineering genius and friend of many years, Michael Jenkins, who wedged himself into tight spaces to help us create a dual system for using both well and city water. Mike also shared his stories of living on Elrod Road in the 1970s.

In our process of learning more about the slough and how to protect it, many people were generous with their time and expertise. The Columbia Slough Watershed Council, formed in the mid-nineties as a citizen-led coordinating council for the slough, is the primary nonprofit that works to increase public awareness, education, and advocacy for a healthy watershed. Kirk Fatland, former volunteer coordinator for the council, was especially helpful to us, and we enjoyed partnering with his volunteers on Buffalo slope revegetation projects.

In learning about the history of the slough, we found Ellen Stroud's work immensely informative. An environmental historian and educator, Stroud wrote a seminal 1999 article on the slough that offered important societal and historical contexts for this much-maligned waterway.

An afternoon chat with Linda and Gretchen, the daughters of Albert and Leona Giese, provided detail for several chapters about our home and its early years. Their photos and clippings of themselves, their parents and friends were precious resources and gifts.

Thanks also to our longtime friends who featured in the story of the gas and water line fiasco. They will recognize the story (and we hope get a laugh from it), but we chose to change their names to protect their privacy.

Many City of Portland employees provided us information about slough conditions and efforts to improve them. At the Bureau of Environmental Services, we thank Nancy Hendrickson and Susan Barthel, long time advocates and coordinators of slough remediation efforts. At the Bureau of Planning and Sustainability, Mindy Brooks and Dan Soebbing gave us a helpful 101 on golf courses and Portland's zoning strategies. Morgan Steele at the Bureau of Development Services was uber-responsive to our ongoing requests for development plans and updates.

Laura Guderyahn, Portland Parks' natural areas coordinator (and resident turtle expert), and Sarah Miller, project manager at Oregon Department of Environmental Quality, helped us understand and write about a successful slough remediation project.

Portland Audubon is a key driver protecting birds, wildlife, and the natural environments that protect them in our city. We were continuously inspired by the efforts of Bob Sallinger, Audubon's longtime, recently retired conservation director. Bob is the guy who showed up after hours at city planning meetings year after year to advocate and testify for nature. We also thank another longtime birder, Andy Frank, who introduced us to ebird.org, where Andy has logged many species in our area. Andy regularly stops by the Buffalo Slough, and we count on him to identify those small brown birds that look like so many others!

Mike Houck's *Wild in the City* inspired us to seek out the wild and wooly side of the slough. Mike is a local icon who for nearly 40 years has advocated for the preservation of green spaces in Portland's urban neighborhoods.

Prologis, as an international developer of industrial logistics real estate, could have seemed like an enemy when the company bought the Broadmoor Golf Course. But instead, we found their leadership, staff, and contractors to be universally responsive, informative, and helpful. In particular, Ken Barnhart and Jake Maxwell at Prologis have kept us informed at every stage of development and ensured that any issues brought to them were addressed. We've appreciated the good humor and in-person chats with Brandon Luelling, superintendent at Tapani, Prologis' engineering contractor. Tapani is the company to hire when you need to build a very tall wall of earth.

John van Staveren, president and senior scientist at Pacific Habitat Services, has been an ongoing source of expertise and information on how a golf course becomes a wetlands preserve. Pacific Habitat Services under contract with Prologis, oversees the environmental assessment and wetlands engineering of what will become Broadmoor Park. We especially appreciate John's walking the property with us to discuss slough slopes and plantings.

Broadmoor Golf Course and its groundkeepers were our next door neighbors for a dozen years. We had many garden-side conversations with Steve Krieger, course superintendent, who allowed Bruce to plant the borders of our shared property. Steve is the great-grandson of one of the six sisters who created the Broadmoor Golf Course in 1931. A course that for nearly ninety years offered affordable golfing to all the public, Broadmoor is missed by many.

We'd like to thank our longtime neighbors, Karen and Dan and Jan and Tim. Dan shared stories about the Gieses with us and keeps us supplied with fresh fish, elk and venison. Tim donated many downed trees to our landscaping projects, sawing trunks and limbs to manageable sizes. Jan, whose mother lived in the "barn" house, shared garden plums, pears, and Vanport flood photos with us. Karen is our neighborhood's eyes and ears, the first to sight every unusual bird and otter visit.

We are indebted to our longtime family friends, Virginie and David, Laura and Kevin, and Anna and Luke. The clan of Carlsmiths, Fosters and McKees have been the quintessence of friendship over many years, and not just in the fun times swimming, hiking, traveling and more, but in-those-swooping-in-to-help times when help is sorely appreciated.

Locally owned plant nurseries have provided invaluable gardening advice. Richard and Lori Vollmer—owners of Garden Fever—have been particularly helpful. Richard even made a free house call to repair our broken outdoor fountain. Ernie Marbott, of Marbott's Nursery on Columbia Blvd. told us many stories about the "old days" when his father began the business during the Great Depression. Ernie passed in 2022 at age ninety-three. Also, many thanks to his wife Connie and son Larry. Portland Nursery—an institution of Stump City—has never failed to provide tiptop service and gardening expertise.

Lori Basson enriched our knowledge of native plants. The former owner of Camamu Soap, she is an expert in ethnobotany. Lori walked our property, identifying many plants and explaining their nutritional and medicinal uses. We learned from her about the poisonous monkshood (*Aconitum napellus*) in our flower garden, once used in Europe to poison wolves.

Special thanks to the indefatigable Pete Botke, owner of Buds Expert Tree Care. He and his crew have pruned and/or taken down many damaged trees on our property. He has also provided hundreds of yards of high-quality free chips for our garden. Pete has a sharp eye for spotting wildlife, a soft heart for endangered bird nests, and an insider's knowledge about what's happening on the Columbia Slough.

In deciding to shape our musings about the slough and our home into a book, we were encouraged by our author friends, Judy Blankenship and Laura O. Foster. They commented on several drafts and suggested many improvements. Judy, now a co-publisher at Aristata Press, introduced us to Anne McClard, her fellow co-publisher, and together the two convinced us we had a publishable book. Nonprofit presses like Aristata enable more authors to find audiences and more readers to find books that aren't crafted specifically to meet the latest market trend. Our city is much richer for this resource.

Sharon AvRutick, our diligent, uber-thorough and thoughtful copy editor, helped us see where fewer words were more, and where more words were needed for someone not from Portland to visualize our locale. Amanda Williams' pen and ink talent and eye for plant, animal, and geographic details resulted in the unique maps, cover, and illustrations that brought our home, its plants, and animals to life.

Our friend of thirty years, Shoshana (Sho) Blauer took many walks with us here in every season. Sho and Nancy biked the Marine Drive path, walked the Elrod Canal on a day it froze, and traversed the entire golf course shortly after closing, gaping at the fallen sequoias. Sho's husband Stephen Miller, an avid kayaker and slough volunteer, paddles up the Buffalo when there's enough water. Our dear friend Shoshana passed away Christmas Day, 2022. We'll hold her in our hearts forever.

Finally, we thank Jeremy Campbell, Willow Crum, and Miranda Acharya (and their spouses, Nicole Campbell, Eric Crum, and Athul Acharya). We are so fortunate to have these six adults and their families in our lives. They enliven every dinner party with their wicked funny satire and stories, sharing our love for home and family, and passion for hiking, gardening, and the natural world. This book is really for them.

SELECTED REFERENCES

PROLOGUE

Original Journals of the Lewis and Clark Expedition. 1804-1806. Wisconsin Historical Society Digital Library and Archives. Wisconsin Historical Society 2003.

Ronda, James P. 1984. *Journals of the Lewis and Clark Expedition*, Ch. 7. Lewis and Clark among the Indians: Down the Columbia. University of Nebraska Press Lincoln and London, 1984. 9 July 2019, https://lewisandclarkjournals.unl.edu/item/lc.-sup.ronda.01.07.

Rose, Mary. "Important Foods: Wapato." 8 April 2016. *Confluence Library*, http://www.confluenceproject.org/library-post/important-foods-wapato/.

"Wapato Valley Oregon Encyclopedia, Oregon Historical Society, 10 Aug. 2019, https://www.oregonencyclopedia.org/articles/wappato_indians/#.Y4Op8i-B1uV.

CHAPTER ONE

"About the Watershed," *Columbia Slough Watershed Council*, 8 Aug. 2019, https://www.columbiaslough.org/about-the-watershed.

CHAPTER TWO

Naskar, Abhijit. "When Veins Ignite: Either Integration or Degradation." Independently published, 12 March, 2021.

CHAPTER THREE

"Columbia Blvd Wastewater Treatment Plant." Portland.gov, 10 Sep. 2019, https://www.portland.gov/service-locations/columbia-boulevard-wastewater-treatment-plant.VIEW 74:65-95 1999.

"Protecting Rivers and Streams." Portland.gov, Environmental Services, 9 Sep. 2019, https://www.portland.gov/bes/protecting-rivers-streams/portlands-watersheds/columbia-slough.

Stroud, Ellen. "Troubled Waters in Ecotopia: Environmental Racism in Portland, Oregon." 1999, MIT. *Radical History Review,* 74:65-95.

"Sunderland Neighborhood." Central Northeast Neighbors, 12 Sep. 2019, https://cnncoalition.org/neighborhoods/sunderland/.

CHAPTER FOUR

Adams, Jeff. "A Bug's Life—Handbook of Aquatic Invertebrates and Macroinvertebrate Monitoring in the Columbia Slough. Xerces Society for Invertebrate Conservation, June 2006, 21 March 2021, https://digital.osl.state.or.us/islandora/object/osl%3A16427/datastream/OBJ/view.

"Columbia Slough Watershed Report Card." Portland.gov, Environmental Services, 7 February 2022, https://www.portland.gov/bes/protecting-rivers-streams/portlands-watershed-report-cards/columbia-slough-watershed-report.

Friedman, Ashley. "The Decibel Level of Normal Speech." The Classroom, 12 May 2022, https://www.theclassroom.com/decibel-level-normal-speech-8599569.html.

Hilary Temple, Amanda. "Wildlife Connectivity Modeling for the Northern Red-legged Frog in the Portland Metropolitan Area, Oregon." Portland State University PDX Scholar, 5 May 2020, https://pdxscholar.library.pdx.edu/open_access_etds/5432/.

"How Loud is Construction Site Noise?" American National Standards Institute, 3 June 2021, https://blog.ansi.org/2018/10/how-loud-is-construction-site-noise/#gref.

"Noise Level Comparisons: F-35 and Other Aircraft." Safe Skies Clean Water Wisconsin, 6 June 2020, https://www.safeskiescleanwaterwi.org/noise-level-comparisons-f-35-and-other-aircraft/.

Pemberton, Ryan. "Shifting Wetland Policy and Perception in the Columbia Slough." PDX Scholar, Portland State University, 2017, https://pdxscholar.library.pdx.edu/cgi/viewcontent.cgi?article=1021&context=geog_masterpapers.

Radle, Autumn Lynn. "The Effect of Noise on Wildlife: A Literature Review." University of Oregon graduate paper, 3 March 2007, https://winapps.umt.edu/winapps/media2/wilderness/toolboxes/documents/sound/radle_effect_noise_wildlife.pdf.

"The 3 Poisonous Spiders Found in Oregon." Bird Watching.com, 14 April 2022, https://birdwatchinghq.com/poisonous-spiders-in-oregon/.

CHAPTER SIX

"Analysis of Refinery Chemical Emission and Health Effects." Office of Environmental Health Hazard Assessment, 27 April 2021, https://oehha.ca.gov/media/downloads/faqs/refinerychemicalsfacts032019.pdf.

"Risk Assessments for Toxic Air Pollutants: A Citizen's Guide." United States Environmental Protection Agency, 5 March 2021, https://www3.epa.gov/airtoxics/3_90_024.html.

"ToxFAQs for Polychlorinated Biphenyls (PCBS)." Agency for Toxic Substances and Disease Registry, 7 June 2021, https://wwwn.cdc.gov/TSP/ToxFAQs/ToxFAQsDetails.aspx?faqid=140&toxid=26.

CHAPTER EIGHT

"Natural Resources Inventory: Riparian Corridors and Wildlife Habitat." Portland.gov, Environmental Services, 2011_05. Middle Columbia Corridor/Airport E-document, 9 Jan. 2020, https://efiles.portlandoregon.gov/record/14139146.

CHAPTER NINE

Glasgow, Leslie L. & McCullough, Yvonne A. "Nutria for Home Use (Circular 77)." April 1963, In cooperation with the Louisiana Wildlife and Fisheries Commission, 12 May 2022, https://nutria.com/wp-content/uploads/NutriaForHomeUse1963recipeBook.pdf.

Miller, Henry. "Eradication by Mastication returns to laid-back roots," Statesman Journal 15 July 2015, 14 May 2022, https://www.statesmanjournal.com/story/travel/outdoors/2015/07/16/eradication-mastication-returns-laid-back-roots/30168771/.

"Nutria, an Invasive Rodent." United States Dept of Agriculture, 12 May 2022, https://www.aphis.usda.gov/publications/wildlife_damage/fsc-nutria-invasive-rodent.pdf.

"Nutria (Myocastor coypus)." Washington Det of Fish and Wildlife, 12 May, 2022, https://wdfw.wa.gov/species-habitats/invasive/myocastor-coypus.

"South Korea's Latest Food Craze: Gigantic Rodents?" Visit Korea Expose 12 May 2022, https://koreaexpose.com/korea-food-crazy-gigantic-rodent-nutria/.

CHAPTER TEN

"Black Cottonwood." The Wood Database, 3 June 2022, https://www.wood-data base.com/black-cottonwood/.

"Black Cottonwood (Populus trichocarpa)." Oregon Innovative Wood Center, 3 June 2022, https://wood.oregonstate.edu/black-cottonwood-populus-trichocarpa.

Cantor, Cliff. "It's snowing . . .fluffy seeds of black cottonwood." Tree Pacific NW28, May 2017, 17 June 2022, https://www.treespnw.com/resources/snowing-cotton wood-seeds.

"Cottonwood III." The Butler Institute of Modern Art, 17 June 2022, https://butlerart.com/portfolio-item/cottonwood-iii/.

"Maynard Dixon." BYU Museum of Art, 17 June 2022, https://moa.byu.edu/maynard-dixon.

O'Shea, Ellen. "Black Cottonwood and the Balm of Gilead." Cascadia Now! 12, April 2017, 27 May 2021, https://www.cascadianow.org/articles/black-cotton wood-and-the-balm-of-gilead.

"Placement is Key for Cottonwood Trees." Beaver Tree Services Inc., 3 June 2022, https://beavertree.net/blog/placement-is-key-for-cottonwood-trees/.

"The Cottonwood's Hidden Secret is a Star." United Country Real Estate, 27 May 2021, https://www.buyheritage.com/articles/land-for-sale/the-cotton woods-hidden-secret-is-a-star-.

CHAPTER ELEVEN

Barthel, Susan. Columbia Slough Program Coordinator. Personal Interview. July 2014.

CHAPTER TWELVE

"3Billion Birds Gone." American Bird Conservancy 17 Feb. 2021, https://abcbirds.org/3-billion-birds/.

"BES Flyway Wetlands Enhancement." Green Works, 11 Sept. 2022, https://greenworkspc.com/ourwork/2018/6/19/bes-flyway-wetlands-enhancement.

"Columbia Children's Arboretum." Portland.gov, 9 Jan. 2023, https://www.portland.gov/parks/columbia-childrens-arboretum.

Daley, Jim. "American Birds Have Vanished." Scientific American 19 Sept. 2019, 17 Feb. 2021, https://www.scientificamerican.com/article/silent-skies-billions-of-north-american-birds-have-vanished/.

Gervais, Jennifer & Rosenberg, Daniel. "Conservation Assessment for The Western Painted Turtle in Oregon." U.S.D.I, Bureau of Land Management, and Fish and Wildlife Service, U.S.D.A., Forest Service Region 6, Oregon Department of Fish and Wildlife, City of Portland, Metro, August 2009, 19 Feb. 2021, https://www.portlandoregon.gov/bes/article/273016.

"Northern Flicker Life History." All About Birds 16 Feb. 2021, https://www.allaboutbirds.org/guide/Northern_Flicker/lifehistory.

"Northern Flicker." American Bird Conservancy 17 Feb. 2021, https://abcbirds.org/bird/northern-flicker/.

"Sunderland Neighborhood Guide." Portland Neighborhood.com 9 August 2022, 18 Feb. 2021, https://portlandneighborhood.com/sunderland.

Wood, Shelby. "Calculate, compare neighborhood "walkability" with Walk Score." The Oregonian, 18 July 2008, 18 Feb. 2021, https://www.oregonlive.com/pdxgreen/2008/07/walkscore.html.

CHAPTER FOURTEEN

Atkinson, Rob. "Animal Folklore: A Mole in the Hand." Folklore Thursday 17, April 2017, 11 Jan. 2022, https://folklorethursday.com/folklife/animal-folklore-mole-hand/.

Bostock, John, et al. "The Natural History. Pliny the Elder, Chap. 7(3.)—Opinions of the Magicians Relative to the Mole. Five Remedies Derived From It." Taylor and Francis, Red Lion Court, Fleet Street, 1855, 11 Jan. 2022, https://www.perseus.tufts.edu/hopper/text?doc=Perseus%3Atext%3A1999.02.0137%3Abook%3D30%3Achapter%3D7.

Delong, William. "The Story of the Zoologist Who Ate Everything—Including the King's Heart." All That's Interesting 22 December 2017, 11 Jan. 2022, https://allthatsinteresting.com/william-buckland.

Pierce, Robert A. "Controlling Nuisance Moles." Extension University of Missouri. 27 January 2015, 1 Feb. 2022, https://extension.missouri.edu/publications/g9440.

"The Mole People." Turner Classic Movies, 2023, 10 Jan. 2022, https://www.tcm.com/tcmdb/title/83815/the-mole-people/#overview.

"The U.S. Military and the Herbicide Program in Vietnam." National Library of Medicine, 1994, 22 Jan. 2022, https://www.ncbi.nlm.nih.gov/books/NBK236347/.

Timmer, David. "Scapanus townsendii." Animal Diversity Web 2004, 10 Jan. 2022, https://animaldiversity.org/accounts/Scapanus_townsendii/.

CHAPTER FIFTEEN

City of Portland, Bureau of Environmental Services and GSI Water Solutions Inc., *Columbia Slough Sediment Data Analysis Report.* Prepared for Oregon Department of Environmental Quality, June 2018, 12 Dec. 2019.

CHAPTER SIXTEEN

"American Crow." National Audubon Society, 2023, 7 Feb. 2023, https://www.audubon.org/field-guide/bird/american-crow.

Gardener, James Ross. "Why Are Crows Committing Acts of Necrophilia?" The New York Times, 19 July 2018, 11 March 2022, https://www.nytimes.com/2018/07/19/science/crows-necrophilia.html.

"Huginn & Muninn." Hrafn Gin18 February 2020, 14 Oct. 2022, https://www.hrafngin.com/post/huginn-and-muninn.

Saxena, Ritesh. "Do Crows Eat Other Birds. Truth Revealed," Earth Life, 27 September 2022, https://earthlife.net/birds/do-crows-eat-other-birds.

Wu, Catherine J. "It's Not Without Caws That Crows Desecrate Their Dead." Smithsonian Magazine 20 July 2018, 11 March 2022, https://www.smithsonianmag.com/science-nature/necrowphilia-180969708/.

CHAPTER SEVENTEEN

City of Portland Bureau of Environmental Services and GSI Water Solutions Inc., *Columbia Slough Fish Tissue Report. 2015 Sampling.* Prepared for Oregon Department of Environmental Quality. 2018 revision, 5 Jan 2020.

Learn, Scott. "Columbia Riverkeeper tests toxics in fish destined for fisherman's tables." The Oregonian. October 18, 2012.

Markowitz, G., Rosner, D. Monsanto, PCBs, and the creation of a "world-wide ecological problem".*J Public Health Pol*39, 463–540 (2018). 10 Jan 2020, https://doi.org/10.1057/s41271-018-0146-8.

CHAPTER EIGHTEEN

Arsenault, Chris. "Only 60 Years of Farming Left If Soil Degradation Continues." Scientific American, 5 December 2014, 7 March 2022, https://www.scientificamerican.com/article/only-60-years-of-farming-left-if-soil-degradation-continues/.

Dykes, Allanah. "The Different Types of Clay Soil—And How to Work with Them." Hunker, 3 October 2021, 1 Nov. 2022, https://www.hunker.com/12003887/different-types-of-clay-soil.

"Hunter Gatherers: Ancient Diets and Modern Man." Union Kitchen, 22 Nov. 2022, https://www.unionkitchen.com/resources/hunter-gatherers-ancient-diets-and-modern-man.

McSheehy, Jill. "7 Organic Pesticides and Their Uses." The Beginner's Garden, 8 June 2020, 3 Nov. 2022, https://journeywithjill.net/gardening/2020/06/08/organic-pesticides-how-to-use/.

"Missoula Floods. The Columbia River—A Photographic Journey," 7 January 2021, 29 Dec. 2022, http://columbiariverimages.com/Regions/Places/missoula_floods.html.

Narsaria, Anupriya. "How Is Soil Formed and How Many Layers Does It Have?" Science ABC, 22 January 2022, 5 March 2022, https://www.scienceabc.com/nature/how-is-soil-formed-and-how-many-layers-does-it-have.html.

Norris, Phil. "From Modern Mummies to Fantasy Coffins, 9 Death Rituals From Around the World." Matador Network, 21 October 2019, 13 Feb. 2023, https://matadornetwork.com/read/death-rituals-around-world/.

Rendall, Heather. "An Old Gypsy Tale or The Possible Origins of the 'Trees." Worcestershire Record No. 25 p. 25-26, 25 November 13 Feb. 2023, https://www.wbrc.org.uk/worcrecd/Issue%2025/an_old_gypsy_tale_or_the_possibl.htm.

Roosevelt, Franklin D. "The nation that destroys its soil destroys itself." 26 February 1937 Letter to State Governors, 2 Feb. 2023, https://www.plymouth.ac.uk/news/pr-opinion/the-nation-that-destroys-its-soil-destroys-itself.

Sapkota, Anupama. "Microorganisms found in soil with effects and examples." Microbe Notes, 1 June 2022, 9 July 2022, https://microbenotes.com/microorganisms-in-soil/.

CHAPTER TWENTY

"April 3, 1806—Lewis & Clark Expedition." University of Portland Clark Library, 23 Jan. 2022, https://sites.up.edu/museum/april-3-1806-lewis-and-clark-expedition/.

Azuma, Elichiro "*In This Great Land of Freedom: The Japanese Pioneers of Oregon,*" Chapter 3: "Development of Japanese Farming Communities," Japanese American National Museum, 1993.

Bradley, Haillie. "Seoullo 7017: Where to Walk in Seoul, Korea." 23 Jan. 2022, https://thesoulofseoul.net/seoullo7017/.

Pavid, Katie. "What is the Anthropocene and Why Does it Matter?" Natural History Museum, 14 Dec. 2022, https://www.nhm.ac.uk/discover/what-is-the-anthropocene.html.

"Prologis." 31 Dec. 2021, https://www.prologis.com/sustainability/environmental-stewardship.

"The High Line." Visit New York City Parks and Recreation 9 May 2020, 23 Jan. 2022, https://www.nycgovparks.org/parks/the-high-line.

CHAPTER TWENTY-ONE

"Lower Columbia Slough Refugia Engineered Log Jams." City of Portland Environmental Services. 20 Nov. 2020, https://www.portlandoregon.gov/bes/article/633543.

Rosenberg, Daniel, and Jennifer Gervais. "Conservation Plan for Native Turtles in the Columbia Slough." V. 1.0, Oregon Wildlife Institute, July 2012. Prepared for the City of Portland and Oregon Department of Environmental Quality. 12 Nov. 2020, http://www.oregonwildlife.org/documents/turtle_plan_columbia_ju ly2012.pdf.

CHAPTER TWENTY-TWO

"Bird of the Week: Western Tanager." Cascade Loop 21 May 2019, 12 April 2021, https://www.cascadeloop.com/articles/bird-of-the-week-western-tanager.

Malka, Stacy. "Glyphosate: Cancer and other Health Concerns." U.S. Right to Know, 9 Feb. 2023, https://usrtk.org/pesticides/glyphosate-health-concerns/.

"Sacred Trees: Arbutus (Madrone) Tree." Arbutus Arts. Com, 11 April 2021, https:// www.arbutusarts.com/sacred-trees.html.

CHAPTER TWENTY-THREE

"Discover a new world of birding." eBird, The Cornell Lab of Ornithology, 6 Dec. 2021, https://ebird.org/home.

Ghosh, Upal; Luthy, Richard G.; Cornelissen, Gerard; Werner, David; Menzie, Charles A.

"In-situ Sorbent Amendments: A New Direction in Contaminated Sediment Management."

Environmental Science & Technology 2011), 45(4), 1163-1168CODEN: ESTHAG; ISSN:0013-936X. (American Chemical Society), 2 Dec. 2021, https://pubs.acs.org/ doi/10.1021/acs.est.7b05114.

Guderyahn, Laura, Ecologist. Portland Parks and Recreation. Personal Interview, 22 Nov. 2021.

"Guidance for the Identification and Control of Safety and Health Hazards in Metal Scrap Recycling."US Occupational Safety and Health Administration, 6 Dec. 2021, https://www.osha.gov/sites/default/files/publications/OSHA3348-metal-scrap-recycling.pdf.

Miller, Sarah. OR Department of Environmental Quality Clean-up Program. Personal Interview. 16, Nov. 2021.

RECORD OF DECISION For Metro Metals Northwest, Inc. Portland, Oregon, ECSI# 5455, Prepared By Oregon Department of Environmental Quality Northwest Region Office, January 2016, 3 Dec. 2021, https://www.deq.state.or.us/Webdocs/Controls/Output/PdfHandler.ashx?p=f36e88fb-7f2f-41eb-90c0-2c638570d714pdf&s=5455RecordofDecisionMetroMetalsFinal.pdf.

Van Staveren, John. President, Pacific Habitat Services. Personal interview, 21 July 2020.

"Wetlands Fact Sheet Series." United States Environmental Protection Agency, 5 Dec. 2021, https://www.epa.gov/wetlands/wetlands-factsheet-series.

"Whitaker Ponds Natural Area." Portland.gov, 5 Dec. 2021, https://www.portland.gov/parks/whitaker-ponds-natural-area.

CHAPTER TWENTY-FOUR

"Columbia River A Photographic Journey," 11 October 2022, http://columbiariverimages.com/Regions/Places/columbia_slough.html.

"Emerald Ash Borer Resources." OSU Extension Services, 9 November 2022, https://extension.oregonstate.edu/collection/emerald-ash-borer-resources.

"Killdeer Life History." All About Birds, 8 November 2022, https://www.allaboutbirds.org/guide/Killdeer/lifehistory.

"Spotted Towhee." All About Birds, 8 November 2022, https://www.allaboutbirds.org/guide/Spotted_Towhee/overview.

ABOUT THE AUTHORS

NANCY HENRY grew up along lakes and rivers in the South, where she developed a love for open water. For many years, she led a creative team that designed learning programs for national service and educational clients. Currently, she lives in Portland, Oregon, where she bikes, swims, gardens and volunteers.

BRUCE CAMPBELL lives in Portland, Oregon, where he gardens, hikes, and writes short stories, novels, and nonfiction. Published in *The Timberline Review, Aestas 2015,* and *The Tishman Review,* Bruce was a two-time award winner in Willamette Writers' Kay Snow Fiction Contest and a finalist in the San Francisco Writers Conference Contest and the Tucson Festival of Books.

SELECT ARISTATA PRESS TITLES

LEAVINGS: Memoir of a 1920s Hollywood Love Child, by Megan McClard, 2022

Spanish language edition of: *Tell Mother I'm in Paradise: Memoirs of a Political Prisoner in El Salvador* by Ana Margarita Gasteazoro—*Díganle a mi madre que estoy en el paraíso: Memorias de una prisionera política en El Salvador,* Edited by Judy Blankenship and Andrew Wilson, 2022.

COMING IN 2023

This Rough Magic: At Home on the Columbia Slough, by Nancy Henry and Bruce Campbell, illustrated by Amanda Williams, August 2023.

Butterfly Dreams: a Novel, by Anne McClard, August 2023.

Women Caught in the Crossfire: One Woman's Quest for Peace in South Sudan, by Abuk Jervis Makuac and Susan Lynn Clark, October 2023.

Raising Owen: an Extra-ordinary Memoir on Motherhood, by Suzanne Lezotte, October 2023.

Aristata Press is non-profit organization. We depend on charitable contributions and volunteers to keep the lights on. We are a tax exempt–501(c)(3)–organization (EIN 92-0281706), which means that your contributions are tax deductible. Contributions that we receive will go directly to supporting the publications of deserving literary works by authors that for one reason or another would be unlikely to find a home in the for-profit publishing sector.

Please visit us at: https://aristatapress.com